IMAGES
of America

IDAHO IN
WORLD WAR II

IMAGES
of America

IDAHO IN
WORLD WAR II

Students from Idaho State University's
MGT 4499/5599 Class

ARCADIA
PUBLISHING

Published by Arcadia Publishing
Charleston, South Carolina

Library of Congress Control Number: 2019955965

For all general information, please contact Arcadia Publishing:
Telephone 843-853-2070
Fax 843-853-0044
E-mail sales@arcadiapublishing.com
For customer service and orders:
Toll-Free 1-888-313-2665

Visit us on the Internet at www.arcadiapublishing.com

The authors are, from left to right, Ashley French, Kathryn W. Rose, Sophia Perry, and Dalene Hunter. (Courtesy of Kelsey West.)

CONTENTS

ACKNOWLEDGMENTS

A project of this magnitude is not possible without cooperation and contributions from a variety of sources. We are grateful for the assistance of Trent Clegg and the Marshall Public Library, Lynn Murdoch and the Bannock County Historical Society, the Densho Digital Repository of photographs from the Minidoka Internment National Historic Site, the Museum of North Idaho in Coeur d'Alene, Danielle Grundel and Alisha Graefe of the Idaho State Archives in Boise, and Ian Fennell and Jeff Papworth of the *Idaho State Journal*. We also wish to acknowledge LuAnn Dudunake Spain and the entire Dudunake family; Karen Scow, Ron, and Patty Bolinger; Vaughn and Arita Wagoner; and the dozens of other individuals who shared photographs and stories for this book. Author Sophia Perry would like to thank her grandmother Lucy Perry for instilling in her a love of English and grammar that led her to an interest in this project. Author Kathryn Rose would like to thank her small family—her husband, Josh, and her cat, Frankie—for supporting her as she worked on this project.

Special thanks to Dr. Ron and Patty Bolinger, whose generous financial gift to Idaho State University (ISU) made this project possible. Thanks also to Dr. Neil Tocher and the ISU Department of Management and Marketing and to Dr. Cindy Hill, Dr. Shannon Kobs Nawotniak, and Dr. Jamie Romine-Gabardi of the ISU Honors Program for cosponsoring this course. Thank you to Suzette Porter and Gail Hunt for their administrative support and constant encouragement. We are deeply indebted to our title editor, Angel Hisnanick, and the staff and administrators at Arcadia Publishing for all of their assistance. Finally, we are grateful to Carrie Leavitt and the Idaho State Veterans Home in Pocatello for hosting our class's final presentation and inspiring us by their extraordinary care for our veterans, from the "Greatest Generation" to today.

INTRODUCTION

Idaho may not be the first state that comes to mind as a major contributor to the American war effort in World War II. Many people—Idahoans included—are largely unaware of how big a role the Gem State played in World War II. Despite this unfamiliarity, Idaho citizens contributed on the home front in ways both big and small, visible and largely hidden. In Pocatello, women and children created United Service Organization (USO) huts to provide cookies and coffee for soldiers at the train stop, preparing to head toward the West Coast and the Pacific theater of the war. Decades later, the men who were on the receiving end of these kindnesses still thought fondly of their last stop and taste of home before they abandoned everything they had known to serve their country. In Coeur d'Alene, sailors in training spent precious recreational time playing ping pong and other games with USO volunteers from the community. The newly-famous Sun Valley Ski Resort closed during the later years of the war to serve as a naval convalescent hospital. What is now the Lava Hot Springs Inn in southeastern Idaho was used as a hospital and sanitorium, offering recuperating troops easy access to its naturally warm, medicinal mineral waters. Citizens of all ages, from children to the elderly, provided funds for the war by purchasing war bonds. Families grew "victory gardens" in their backyards so that more of the rationed foods and goods could be sent to the troops to supply the war effort. Entrepreneurs such as Jack Simplot discovered innovative ways of dehydrating Idaho-grown potatoes and onions to ship them as part of troop rations throughout the world.

Idaho's contributions were not limited to the organizing of individual citizens and communities, however. Gowen Field in Boise and nearby Mountain Home Air Base served as training sites for pilots learning to fly and fight the war in the skies. A similar airfield was established in Pocatello, which is now the Pocatello Airport. Near Silver City, in remote central Idaho, the discovery of tungsten in the Stibnite Mines provided the United States with a precious material that allowed their bullets to pierce the armor of the enemy and gain the upper hand in the war. Many people worked in the mines, isolated from their families and homes, but willing to make that sacrifice for the war effort. In the desert northwest of Idaho Falls and Blackfoot, the military tested armaments at the Arco Naval Proving Ground and Bombing Ranges. Occasionally, live ammunition rounds are still found in the desert today.

Even colleges got into the act. Boise State Junior College (now Boise State University) strengthened its pre-medic and pre-nursing programs to help train medical personnel who cared for the wounded. Lewiston Normal College (now Lewis and Clark State University) became one of the largest training centers for naval air cadets in the country. And the University of Idaho Southern Branch (now Idaho State University) in Pocatello hosted the V-12 naval leadership training program. These program innovations not only served the needs of the country, but also saved the colleges from financial insolvency due to so many college-aged students being drafted or volunteering for military service.

The stories in this book are multifaceted and complex, as Idaho was also the site of great hardships and miscarriages of justice during the war. On the unforgiving plain north of Twin Falls, the

US government established the Minidoka War Relocation Camp to detain Japanese Americans against their will and without due process of law. Furthermore, both German and Italian prisoners of war were held captive, with many of them unable to speak English and constantly afraid for their lives. Some 2,500 detainees and unrecorded numbers of prisoners of war labored to farm and harvest crops of potatoes and sugar beets, which was necessary because so many men were away at war. Sixty thousand Idahoans, nearly 11 percent of the state's population, served in the war, and tragedy touched practically every community in every corner of the state, forever changing the dynamic of the state and its people. Of those 60,000, a total of 1,419 gave the ultimate sacrifice for their country, with many more sustaining life-altering injuries from their time in the service. Yet through it all, Idahoans persevered, and the institutions, physical structures, and stories that persist from that era serve as reminders of their courage, resourcefulness, and abiding sense of community.

This book was written by four students at Idaho State University in fulfillment of the requirements of a semester-long class on collaborative creativity and teamwork. The authors took responsibility for finding and selecting photographs from a variety of historical repositories and other sources throughout the state of Idaho. They then wrote captions that tell the unique stories associated with each of these photographs.

Ashley French is a junior majoring in healthcare administration. Following finishing her bachelor's degree, she is planning on getting a master's in business administration and a master's in healthcare administration.

Dalene Hunter is a junior majoring in anthropology with a minor in English literature. She will be studying abroad in the spring semester of 2020 in Plymouth, England. She has plans to attend graduate school in the fall of 2021 in pursuit of a PhD in anthropology.

Sophia Perry is a senior double majoring in business marketing and management. Additionally, she is pursuing a double minor in Spanish and professional writing. She will graduate with her bachelor's degree in May 2020 and has plans to pursue a master's in business administration.

Kathryn W. Rose is a junior majoring in professional writing, with a minor in marketing. Additionally, she is pursuing an undergraduate thesis through the honors program at the university.

The book is structured into seven chapters, categorized by themes. The first chapter tells the stories of individuals and groups in Idaho and their contributions to the war effort. The middle three chapters describe the presence of the US military in Idaho: by land, by sea, and by air. The book concludes with poignant photographs from the Minidoka War Relocation Camp and depictions of everyday civilian life in Idaho on the home front. We hope you enjoy this book, which represents the fruits of this project in collaborative creativity.

One

REFLECTING ON THE PAST

U.S. DECLARES WAR

THE POCATELLO TRIBUNE

VOL. XI, NO. 248.   Fair tonight, Tuesday fair in south portion but partly cloudy.   POCATELLO, IDAHO, MONDAY, DECEMBER 8, 1941.   Full leased wire Associated Press   PRICE: 5 CENTS.

AMERICAN FATALITIES 1,500

Two Battleships Go Down In Air Raid On Hawaii

This was the headline in the *Pocatello Tribune* the day after the Japanese attack on Pearl Harbor in 1941. Looking back at this now, it is interesting to see how the headline does not read, "Attack on Pearl Harbor"; instead, the focus is on the lives lost on that terrible day. For the Idaho citizens at the time, the war was real, even if the front lines were thousands of miles away. (Courtesy of the Marshall Public Library.)

Shown here is a little boy with his bicycle in the 1940s. It is important to remember the fear of such children during these hard times, especially on December 7, 1941, the day that the Japanese attacked Pearl Harbor, Hawaii. The *Idaho State Journal* wrote an article about young Adelaide Mcleod from Boise, who shared her story about how she learned about the attack. Mcleod said she was riding her bicycle when a young man stopped her and asked if she knew that the country was at war. Mcleod was confused, but the man continued, saying, "Yes, our country's at war, and we're all going to go fight it." Mcleod said this was a moment she would never forget: the moment when the United States finally joined the war. (Courtesy of the Idaho State Archives.)

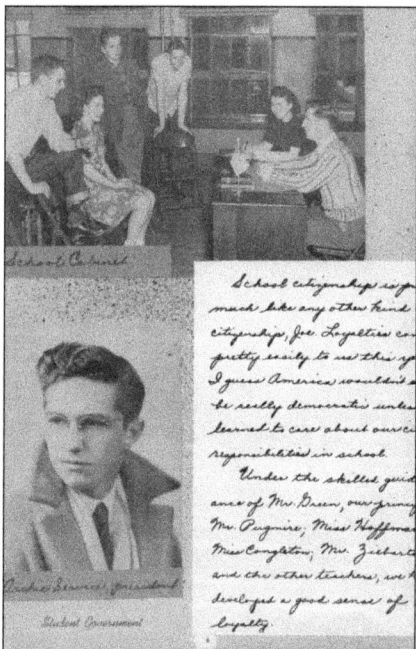

This spread from *The Pocatellian* (Pocatello High School) yearbook features the school's student body president, Archie Service. In World War II, Archie, who was only a young boy at the time, assisted his mother, Edna, by serving cookies and coffee to the soldiers who came through the Pocatello USO huts. Archie's mother went above and beyond in order to help the soldiers feel a little taste of home before heading overseas. Although troop movements via rail were supposed to be secret, Edna talked officials at the train station into letting her know, half an hour in advance, that a train with troops would be arriving in Pocatello so that she could have fresh cookies and coffee ready for them when they arrived. (Courtesy of the Marshall Public Library.)

That's about all I can think of now, Joe. Oh, there were millions of little things that made up the school year: buying war bonds every Wednesday; coming to eight o'clock classes in the pitch darkness of a winter morning; making Red Cross speeches; dancing at the Junior Prom; listening to soldiers back from the theaters of war; writing to friends and relatives in the service.

It's been a serious year, too, Joe. We've tried to be good

The theme of this particular issue of *The Pocatellian* was centered around the students who had been drafted into the war. This collective group of brave students was addressed as Joe, and letters were written throughout the book describing events that had taken place during the time that Joe was away. The students of "Poky High" were anxiously awaiting Joe's safe return and the end of the war that had taken so many loved ones away from them. (Both, courtesy of the Marshall Public Library.)

Americans, so that when you come back, we won't be ashamed to face you — you who have proved that you are good Americans. You're surely a great bunch.

We'll be waiting for you in the old teepee. Come back soon. Poky has the ball in enemy territory now, Joe. I'll meet you at the main gate after we make our final touchdown.

So long, Joe —
Poky High.

Local Boy Seen In Picture of Guadalcanal Sector

Dunn Sends Letter Telling of High Morale of Marines

Mr. and Mrs. Sam A. Dunn, prominent Tyhee residents, have been thrilled by the receipt of a letter from their son Kenneth, who is in the U. S. marine corps, in which he identifies himself as the soldier who appears in a picture published in the Pocatello Tribune sometime ago, depicting an anti-aircraft gun emplacement in the Guadalcanal sector. The Tribune picture showed one soldier man-ning the gun and Mr. Dunn re-ports he identified the soldier as has soon as he saw the paper and forwarded it to Kenneth for confirmation.

Young Dunn's letter indicates the high spirit and morale of the American troops. He writes: "I think those Japs have alre found out just what we are able to do everywher

Commissioning of Bill C. Bond, 22, 1420 South Second street, as a second lieutenant was announc-ed by the U.S. marine corps to-day.

Successful completion of the second phase of his training with the Leathernecks, an eight-week course for officer candidates at Quantico, Va., brought him his gold bars.

He is now in attendance at re-serve officers' class at the same Marine training center, where 10 additional weeks of advanced in-struction will make him eligible for assignment to a combat unit or a specialists' school.

Lieutenant Bond, son of Char-les H. Bond, assistant superinten-dent of Pocatello schools, has been with the Marines since last December, when he began his "boot camp" training at Parris Island, S. C.

Pocatellan Safe

Mr. and Mrs. Frank Anseimo of 525 North Sixth report that rum-ors that their son, Vincent, had been wounded in action at the Solomons, are unconfirmed.

The last letter the Anselmos re-ceived was about six weeks ago. However, Nancy Scardino received a letter Tuesday from her broth-mmy, in which he states ent is safe.
enlisted in the ma-e time and were r in the Sol-Scardino ed at

Private Archie Chandler left Saturday for his station at Camp Campbell, Kentucky, after spend-ing a furlough in Pocatello visit-ing his wife, and mother Mrs. Ada Chandler, 932 South Eighth ave-nue.

Pvt. Reid Bird of the army a corps, is spending a week's fur lough visiting his mother, Mr Mamie Bird, of 934 West Clark Pvt. Bird graduated from th Buckley field armament school b Denver. For the past two month he has served as armer at Foste field, Texas, training center fo advanced air cadets.

Oren 'Bud' Loveland, son of Mr and Mrs. C. J. Loveland, 615 West Young, is on leave from Chicago. He is a radio technician in the navy. He was employed by the telephone company here previous to enlisting.

Pocatellan to Instruct

FORT SILL, Okla.—Sec. Lieu Robert E. Moberly of Pocatell has been assigned as an instruc tor in the department of materia of the field artillery school her Lieutenant Moberly is the so of Maj. and Mrs. E. E. Moberl 1735 Sherman, Denver.

Soldier Returning After Injuries In Solomon Battle

It will be a real Thanksgiving day in the home of Mr. and Mrs. M. J. Dudunake, 552 North Fifth avenue, as their son, John, is coming home next week.

Officially reported "missing in action" in the first engagement in the Solomon islands, John was mourned by relatives and friends until a few weeks ago when word came that he was alive and had been brought to the U. S. hospital in San Diego.

A paratrooper with the n was wound battle. A al sh'

Pocatellans Training

FARRAGUT—Fresh from civil-ian life are the new recruits from Pocatello who are now undergoing intensive training at the U. S.

naval training station, here. Ar-riving recently were: John Davis Powell, jr., son of Mr and Mrs. John D. Powell, 1133 South Fifth, and Lawrence Ray Fowler, son of Mr. and Mrs. N. B. Fowler, 1244 South Fourth.

After a few weeks of rigorous naval training in this wooded Idaho lake-country, the recruits will either be assigned to a service school for additional training in a specialized field or will go to sea on a man-o-war in America's fast-growing fleet.

Navy Awards Cross For John Eversole

WASHINGTON (P)—Nine naval aviation officers who fought in the battle of Midway and are listed as missing have been awarded the navy cross for extraordinary hero-ism.

They include Lt. (JG) John Thomas Eversole, 27, son of Mrs. J. J. Eversole, 137 Roosevelt ave-nue, Pocatello.

The navy announced that each decoration was accompanied by the same citation praising each of-ficer "For extraordinary heroism and courageous devotion to duty while piloting an airplane of a torpedo squadron in action against enemy Japanese forces in the bat-tle of Midway on June 4, 1942."

"Participating in a vigorous and intensive assault against the Jap-anese invasion fleet," the citation continued, "he pressed home attack with relentless determ tion in the face of a terr rage of anti-aircraft f

"The unprecedente under which his a

This is another page taken from the same issue of *The Pocatellian*. Each newspaper clipping mentions a different student involved in the war. From where they were stationed, to awards they had won, to one student even listed as missing in action who eventually returned home, it is clear that this was a school full of brave young students. (Courtesy of the Marshall Public Library.)

This two-page spread from *The Pocatellian* describes in further detail how students of Pocatello High School were involved in the war. Whether it was purchasing war bonds or knitting sweaters for the Red Cross, everyone was helping in some way. Some students even gave the ultimate sacrifice, such as Vernon Nipper (pictured at right), who was the first Idaho youth to give his life in the war. (Both, courtesy of the Marshall Public Library.)

Five Brothers Served In World War II

Three sailors and two soldiers constitute one of Jefferson county's five-star war service families. Five sons of Lester and the late Margaret Hogan Taylor of Lewisville have served in the Navy, Air Force and Army.

At left, above, is Sam Taylor, 31, fireman 2/c, now serving aboard the USS Osmus, a destroyer escort in the Pacific. His wife, Mrs. Olive Griffith Taylor and their two children reside in Rigby.

Gordon Taylor, center, 23, fireman 2/c, served aboard the USS Ranger, CV 4, and was discharged on October 19, 1945. His wife and their 3 children resided in Rigby while he served at sea.

Thomas J. Taylor, 19, was given a medical discharge May 19, 1945. He served aboard a destroyer operating in the Atlantic, having entered the Navy during January, 1944.

S/Sgt. Harry A. Taylor, 21, served in the ETO as a tail gunner on a B-17. He has been stationed at Santa Ana, California since his return from Europe. He entered service in March, 1944.

Pfc. Lester Taylor, Jr., 27, at lower right, went overseas after completing infantry replacement training and was assigned to the Sixth Infantry Division, then in New Guinea. He was wounded in action during the Philippine campaign and returned to the United States for hospitalization. He is now at Madigan hospital, Fort Lewis. His wife, Mrs. Katie Wetzel Taylor, resides in Idaho Falls.

Other Jefferson county families to furnish five sons for war service are Mr. and Mrs. Frank Miller, Sr., of Rirle, and Mr. and Mrs. O. B. Drake of Roberts. In the Miller family there are four sailors and one soldier; the same is true of the Drake family. Of the fifteen men in the three five-star families, eleven are sailors and four soldiers.

Arnold Jack Taylor entered Air Force Oct. 21, 1946, took basic training at Sar Field, San Antonio, Tex. He attended control tower operations school at Scott Field, Belleville, Ill. He graduated May 1947 as honor student assigned to airways and communicator services, served on Okinawa from June 10, 1947 to Jan. 3, 1949. His last assignment was at Hill Field, Ogden, Utah. He was discharged Sept. 17, 1949 as a sergeant.

Goes to Korea

Cpl. David H. Taylor, husband of Mrs. Elizabeth Taylor, Rexburg, processed here with the 3149th Personnel Processing Group enroute to Korea, a news release states.

Before entering the Army in November 1951, Cpl. Taylor was employed as a truck driver.

He is the seventh son of the late Mr. and Mrs. Lester Taylor of Rigby, to serve overseas.

Pictured here is a selection of newspaper clippings telling the stories of the Taylor boys who served in the Navy, Army, and Air Force from the early 1940s to the late 1950s. The five men pictured in the top clipping—Sam Taylor (top left), Gordan Taylor (top center), Thomas J. Taylor (top right), Sgt. Harry A. Taylor (bottom left), and Pfc. Lester Taylor (bottom right)—all served in or around World War II. Their service meant a great deal to their communities and their families in Idaho. (Courtesy of Vaughn and Arita Wagoner.)

Thomas Eugene Bolinger is pictured here in his military uniform near the end of the war in the mid-1940s. As a young man, Bolinger made his way from Arkansas to the western United States, where he served as a ranch hand near the Idaho-Wyoming border. Bolinger was drafted even before the Japanese attack on Pearl Harbor and served under legendary general Douglas McArthur as a mechanic, repairing damaged military vehicles behind the front lines. Turning down the opportunity to go to officer candidate school after the war, Bolinger was able to put the skills that he learned in the military to good use in civilian life. He ultimately settled with his family in Twin Falls, Idaho, where he worked as a mechanic for Molyneaux Machinery and then the Twin Falls Canal Company. (Courtesy of Ron Bolinger.)

Ken Jaeger enjoys a light moment on horseback during the war. Born and raised in Idaho Falls, Jaeger joined the Army and served with the 97th Infantry in Czechoslovakia. After the war, he returned to his father's farm north of Idaho Falls before going to work with the Bureau of Reclamation. He followed that with a stint in the Peace Corps, teaching farming and irrigation techniques in eastern Pakistan. Known for his sense of humor, Jaeger would call home to his parents during the war with eye-roll-inducing jokes, such as, "I slept like a log last night. Do you know how I could tell? I woke up in the fireplace!" (Courtesy of Karen Scow.)

Two

IDAHO CONTRIBUTIONS

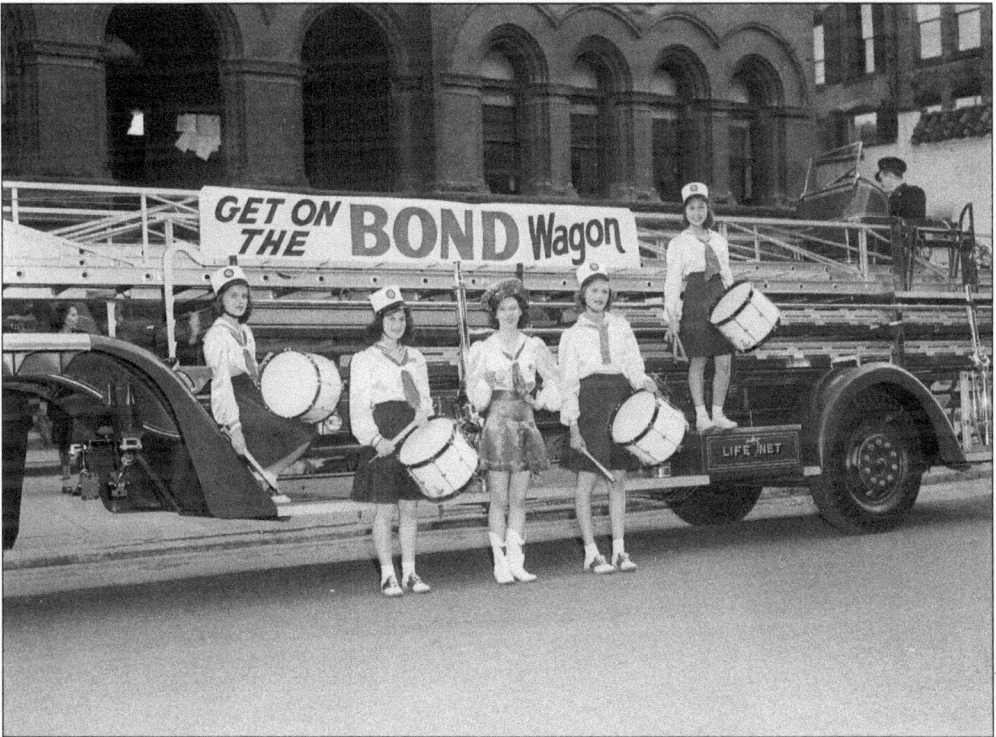

These young women are on a parade float advertising war bonds. Over the course of the war, 85 million Americans purchased approximately $185 million in war bonds, which would be paid back with interest at the conclusion of the war. The US government pulled out all the stops to promote war bonds, enlisting the efforts of Hollywood studios and actors, grassroots parades and rallies such as the event pictured here, and print advertising illustrated by famous portrait artist Norman Rockwell, among others. These girls are posing with their drum majorette, who is the leader of their marching band. This chapter explores the contributions Idaho made to the war effort, from war bonds to Stibnite mines. (Courtesy of the Idaho State Archives.)

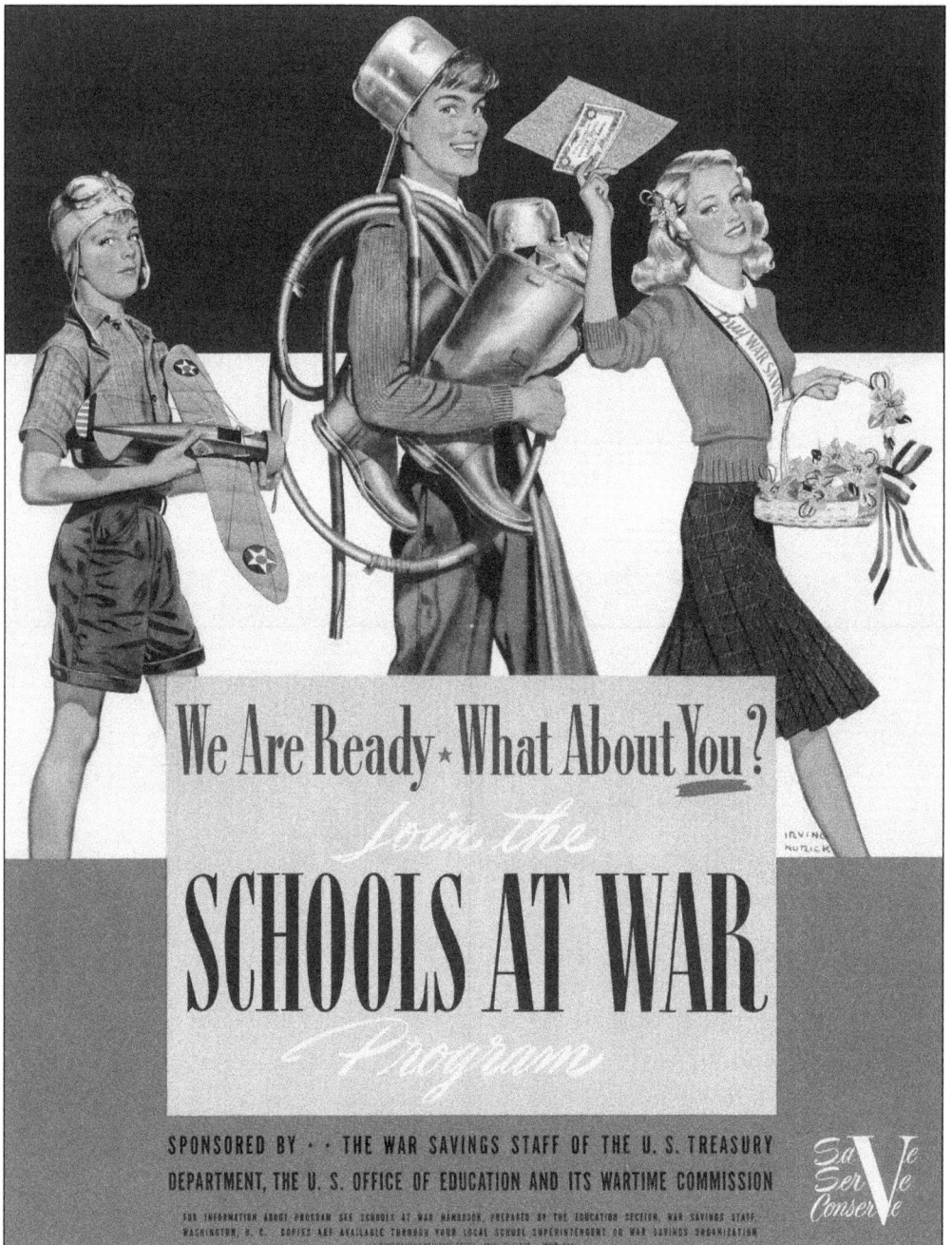

This 1942 poster by Irving Murick advertises the Schools at War program. It shows children aiding in the war effort by preparing for service and selling war bonds. The war savings staff of the US Treasury Department sponsored this program, and its slogan was "save, serve, conserve." (Courtesy of the Idaho State Archives.)

We Are Buying War Bonds 100%

Let us congratulate the Student Body and Faculty on the Third Full Year in the New High School Buildings.

"Let us give our whole attention to the war; let us support by buying saving stamps and bonds; donating to Red Cross; when the war is over, let us plan to rebuild America. At that time come in and see us for plans on your new home. We can arrange all the money and details. All you will have to do is to move in. In the meantime—it is all out for the war and good luck and best wishes to all our boys in the service.

POCATELLO LUMBER CO.

This advertisement from the Pocatello Lumber Company announces that it was purchasing war bonds. Much different than advertisements seen outside of wartime, companies were constantly creating ads such as this one, even though they were not marketing a product or service. They simply showed that companies were supporting the war effort and helped to keep their brand name alive for citizens to remember after the war was over. According to *National Geographic*, "This period of marketing, which began just two months after the U.S. entered World War II, was part of an unprecedented collaboration between advertisers and the U.S. government." (Courtesy of the Marshall Public Library.)

O. P. A. Form No. R-306	UNITED STATES OF AMERICA	Not Valid Before	*5-24-42*
	OFFICE OF PRICE ADMINISTRATION		Date
Serial No. C *38144689*	**SUGAR PURCHASE CERTIFICATE**	TRIPLICATE	

THIS IS TO CERTIFY THAT:

Name: *School Dist No 36* Address:

City: *Kooskia* County: *Idaho* State: *Idaho*

is authorized to accept delivery of *one hundred six* (*106*) pounds of sugar pursuant to Rationing Order No. 3 (Sugar Rationing Regulations) of, and at a price not to exceed the maximum price established by, the Office of Price Administration.

Date *Aug 24, 1942*

Local Rationing Board No. *25*

By *Victor Peterson*
Signature of issuing officer

Idaho *Idaho* *adm*

County State Title

To Be Retained by Original Holder

Above is a certificate that authorized 106 pounds of sugar to be purchased by School District 36 in Kooskia, near the banks of the Clearwater River in north-central Idaho. As food and other goods were in short supply during World War II, many goods such as sugar were rationed. Below is a war ration book issued to Pell Rose in 1944. Individual Americans and families were issued ration books from the US Office of Price Administration. These ration books were required to be able to purchase certain canned foods, fresh foods, and imported foods at the grocer. When an individual used their ration stamps for the month, they would be unable to buy more of that type of food. (Both, courtesy of the Idaho State Archives.)

INSTRUCTIONS

1 This book is valuable. Do not lose it.

2 Each stamp authorizes you to purchase rationed goods in the quantities and at the times designated by the Office of Price Administration. Without the stamps you will be unable to purchase those goods.

3 Detailed instructions concerning the use of the book and the stamps will be issued from time to time. Watch for those instructions so that you will know how to use your book and stamps.

4 Do not tear out stamps except at the time of purchase and in the presence of the storekeeper, his employee, or a person authorized by him to make delivery.

5 Do not throw this book away when all of the stamps have been used, or when the time for their use has expired. You may be required to present this book when you apply for subsequent books.

Rationing is a vital part of your country's war effort. This book is your Government's guarantee of your fair share of goods made scarce by war, to which the stamps contained herein will be assigned as the need arises.

Any attempt to violate the rules is an effort to deny someone his share and will create hardship and discontent.

Such action, like treason, helps the enemy.

Give your whole support to rationing and thereby conserve our vital goods. Be guided by the rule;

"If you don't need it, DON'T BUY IT."

U.S. GOVERNMENT PRINTING OFFICE: 1943 16—30853-1

UNITED STATES OF AMERICA
OFFICE OF PRICE ADMINISTRATION

WAR RATION BOOK TWO
IDENTIFICATION

430149 AE

Pell Rose
(Name of person to whom book is issued)

(Street number or rural route)

Kooskia *Idaho* *52* *f* *430149*
(City or post office) (State) (Age) (Sex)

ISSUED BY LOCAL BOARD No. *25* *Idaho* *Idaho*
(County) (State)
Kooskia
(City)

By *Adele Cravens*
(Signature of issuing officer)

SIGNATURE *Rose Pell by E. M*
(To be signed by the person to whom this book is issued. If such person is unable to sign because of age or incapacity, another may sign in his behalf.)

WARNING

1 This book is the property of the United States Government. It is unlawful to sell or give it to any other person or to use it or permit anyone else to use it, except to obtain rationed goods for the person to whom it was issued.

2 This book must be returned to the War Price and Rationing Board which issued it, if the person to whom it is issued is inducted into the armed services of the United States, or leaves the country for more than 30 days, or dies. The address of the Board appears above.

3 A person who finds a lost War Ration Book must return it to the War Price and Rationing Board which issued it.

4 PERSONS WHO VIOLATE RATIONING REGULATIONS ARE SUBJECT TO $10,000 FINE OR IMPRISONMENT, OR BOTH.

OPA FORM No. R-121 16—30853-1

Pictured above are the Stibnite mines in central Idaho and below are several of the people who worked there during World War II. During the war, the Allied powers faced a crisis when they did not have a source of tungsten for ammunition coating. Italy had made a deal with China to provide the Axis powers with their supply of much-needed tungsten. Thus, the discovery of tungsten at Stibnite represented a monumental breakthrough for the United States and its allies. From this mining contribution alone, the *Washington Post* estimates that Idaho shortened the war by a full year. (Both, courtesy of the Idaho State Archives.)

Pictured above is Silver City, once a haven for miners and speculators and now a famous Idaho ghost town. To the left are the remains of an old mill near Graham, Idaho. Silver mining brought many speculators to Idaho shortly after the Civil War, and boom towns grew quickly around the mines. However, like so many other small mining towns across Idaho, Silver City died soon after all the silver had been mined. During World War II, many of the building materials from structures at Silver City were salvaged for use due to shortages. Today, 75 of the once 300 buildings have survived this salvaging and the test of time. The mill pictured at left, however, did not survive. (Both, courtesy of the Idaho State Archives.)

This image shows US soldiers at a USO event. The USO was founded in 1942 to support US military members and their families during World War II. As servicemen and servicewomen were coming through various parts of the United States, local USO organizers provided them with coffee, cookies, and friendly faces as a taste of home before they shipped out of the country. The USO still helps servicemen and servicewomen today in a variety of ways, including musical tours and the same friendly send-offs seen here. (Courtesy of the Idaho State Archives.)

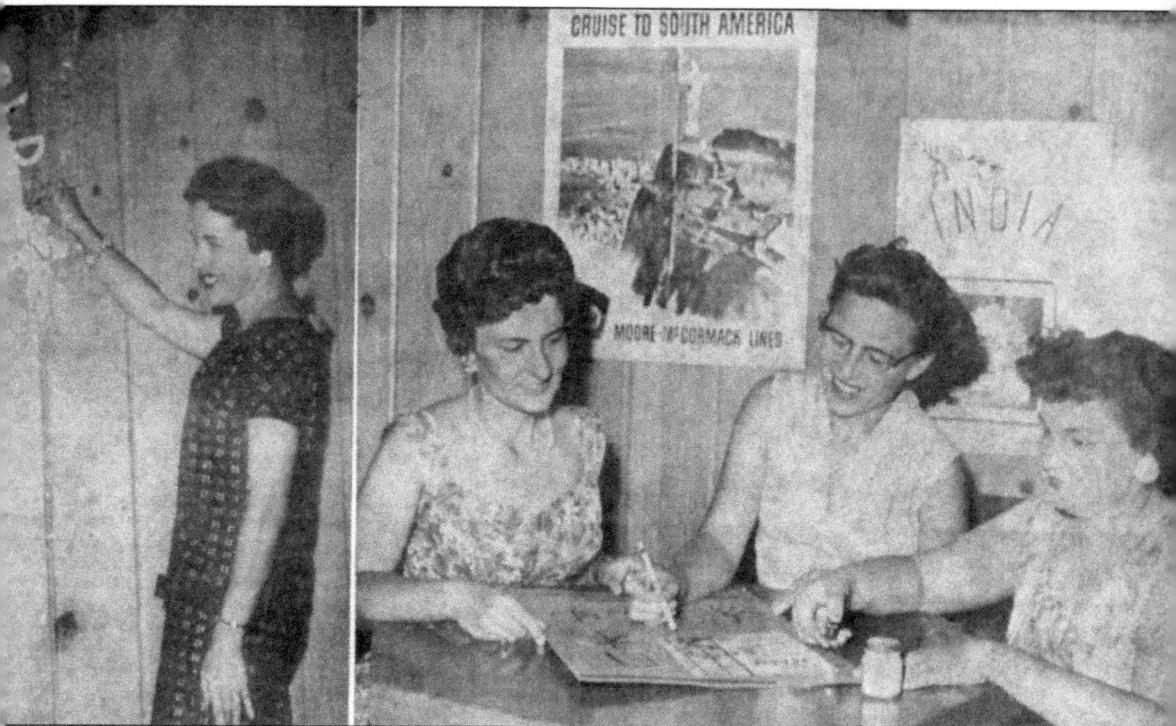

Pictured here are ladies working at the USO hut in Pocatello. As the war progressed, rationing required the women and other contributors at the huts to rework recipes to match the limited ingredients on hand. According to Judy Walker, sugar was rationed very heavily in World War II, along with coffee, meat, cheese, and canned fish. Because of this, the women at the USO huts had to be creative with the cookie recipes they used to serve the soldiers. (Courtesy of the Marshall Public Library.)

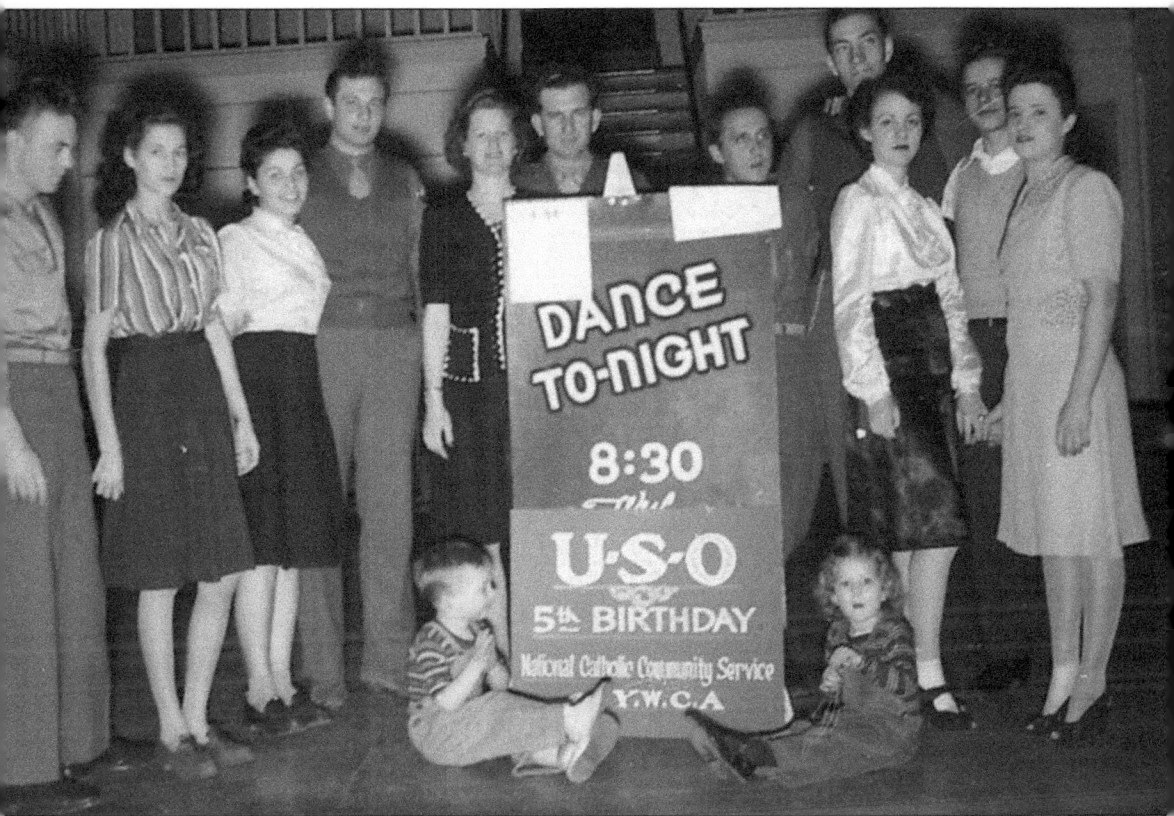

This image shows another example of how the USO was making sure that servicemen riding the trains to be deployed for the war felt welcome before they left everything they knew behind. Other organizations also helped out, including the YWCA and National Catholic Community Service. People from all walks of life came together to support the troops during the war in any way they could, whether that be a victory garden, cookies, or a dance, like this one. (Courtesy of the Idaho State Archives.)

The USO hut in Pocatello became nationally famous. Founded as a railroad town, Pocatello became one of the most diverse cities in the state because of the Oregon Short Line and Union Pacific Railroads, which brought employees and passengers from around the world. The *Pocatello Tribune* noted that the Pocatello USO huts were recognized for their relaxed attitudes toward the diverse ethnic groups passing through town. The men included recent immigrants from many nations, and there was usually someone in Pocatello who could relate to each of them. (Courtesy of the Bannock County Historical Society.)

Here is a view of the Pocatello USO hut during Christmas. These huts became increasingly important during the holiday seasons, a difficult time for soldiers. The troops who came through Pocatello remembered the generosity of the volunteers, who welcomed them with open arms and offered them warmth and comfort during one of the most challenging times of their lives, with letters of gratitude to the citizens of Pocatello still submitted by veterans to the *Idaho State Journal* decades after the war. A collection of some of these letters is currently displayed at the Pocatello Regional Airport. (Courtesy of the Bannock County Historical Society.)

Coeur d'Alene had plans for the recreational facility shown here since 1935. Thanks to the Emergency Relief Appropriation Act passed by the federal government implementing the Works Project Administration (WPA), the plans to create this community center became reality. Basic construction finished in 1939. When the United States entered the war, the construction for the Farragut Navy Training Station had begun, as well as a naval supply depot. The aluminum rolling mill close by provided military members with an off-base place to relax. The Civic Auditorium became the USO-Civic Auditorium and was rapidly filled with sailors. This photograph shows both levels of the interior of the USO building. (Courtesy of the Museum of North Idaho.)

Pictured here is the interior of the USO building near Farragut Navy Training Station, with sailors and hostesses sitting at tables. The second floor offered space for sailors to write letters to family and friends back home. The USO-Civic Auditorium was constantly busy with sailors and other military personnel. It serviced 776,000 recruits in 1943, averaging 2,100 per day. (Courtesy of the Museum of North Idaho.)

Sailors and guests are shown playing ping pong in this USO hut game room in Coeur d'Alene, Idaho. At the USO-Civic Auditorium, there were many activities and places to relax. Sailors spent their time writing letters and dancing to orchestra music. A sister of a former mayor of Coeur d'Alene, Eleanor Smith recalled that "there was no shortage of cute sailors for my best friend Mary Clair Roach and I to dance with. We danced so much that our feet were so swollen, and we walked home barefoot." (Courtesy of the Museum of North Idaho.)

These sailors from the Farragut Naval Training Center are at the USO hut in Coeur d'Alene, standing at the snack bar with the cook seen in the background. Although it is hard to imagine now (only a single building and water tower stands on the site today), Farragut once housed over 700 buildings and boasted a capacity of 45,000 occupants, which would have made it Idaho's largest "city" during the war. Some 300,000 soldiers, officers, employees, and volunteers spent time at Farragut over the course of the war. Due to its proximity to Farragut, this particular snack bar generated a reported $81,000 in revenue in 1943 alone. (Courtesy of the Museum of North Idaho.)

Helen O'Reilly served coffee, donuts, and various other foods daily at the USO-Civic Auditorium snack bar. Here she is seen dispensing Coca-Cola behind the snack bar. According to the Coca-Cola Company, near the beginning of the war, Coca-Cola president Robert Woodruff ordered that "every man in uniform get a bottle of Coca-Cola for five cents, wherever he is and whatever it costs the company." (Courtesy of the Museum of North Idaho.)

The USO-Civic Auditorium commonly had celebrations, dances, and holiday parties for the servicemen and servicewomen. Shown here is a Christmas party for Navy families. A large group of sailors with their wives and children are grouped together, waiting to see Santa. According to an article in *Time* magazine by Eliza Berman, celebrating Christmas during the war was difficult in that many family members were overseas. However, the holidays also brought joy back to these families and offered a welcome distraction. (Courtesy of the Museum of North Idaho.)

The Farragut Naval Training Center was named for Adm. David Glasgow Farragut, a Civil War naval hero who served for 60 years. Farragut became famous during the Battle of Mobile Bay in August 1864 for his order to his ships to advance at full speed despite the presence of "torpedoes" (mines). In the midst of the seriousness of war, Farragut offered fun traditions and opportunities for celebration, such as the one shown here. According to the Idaho Military Museum, one of the more distinctive traditions was a weekly marching and drill competition for possession of a flag depicting a rooster. The rooster flag was a point of pride for the winner, as the members of that company were able to "strut" past other companies on their way to the front of the line at mealtimes. (Courtesy of the Museum of North Idaho.)

A sailor plays for the commanding officer, Captain Hull (right). The opening of Farragut Naval Training Station brought a great deal of attention to northern Idaho. According to the *Spokesman-Review*, the dedication ceremony in August 1942 attracted celebrities and dignitaries, and in one day raised over $45,000 in ticket sales (nearly $730,000 today) for the Navy Relief Fund. Pres. Franklin Roosevelt personally inspected the Farragut site later that fall. (Courtesy of the Museum of North Idaho.)

This crane is harvesting scrap metal in Pocatello. During World War II, every piece of scrap metal able to be recycled was sent away for use in war production. Throughout the United States, people removed the bumpers of their cars and replaced them with wood so they could send the metal away to be repurposed for weapons. (Courtesy of the Bannock County Historical Society.)

This photograph looks toward the south and the "gateway to the Rocky Mountains" with the Union Pacific Railroad tracks cutting through Pocatello. The lack of coordination and continuity in the US railroad system during World War I had substantially hindered the war effort. Although efforts at nationalizing the US railroad system were discontinued after World War I, the improved performance of cross-country rail in the 1920s, 1930s, and early 1940s enabled the transportation of millions of tons of supplies, not to mention thousands of troops, across the nation. Lowell Jackson Thomas, an author, radio commentator, and Presidential Medal of Freedom recipient, lauded that transformation on a radio broadcast on May 12, 1942: "We Americans needed a miracle in railroad transportation . . . and, by George, we got that miracle!" (Courtesy of the Bannock County Historical Society.)

The woman in this photograph is operating a phone at a new facility in Pocatello. During the war, many women worked as phone operators. Men would call their families when they got back to the United States, often surprising them because they were able to contact them before the letters they sent while abroad had arrived back home. (Courtesy of the Bannock County Historical Society.)

This is a celery farm in the Twin Falls area during World War II. Farming was a large part of life in Idaho during the war. Magic Valley in south-central Idaho, with its lower elevations and longer growing seasons than other parts of the state, played a critical role in providing crops ranging from wheat and barley to green beans and corn. The farm seen in this photograph, taken by Twin Falls photographer Clarence Bisbee, was especially lucrative for its time, reportedly bringing in around $1,000 an acre. (Courtesy of the Idaho State Archives.)

The J.L. Kraft cheese plant moved from San Francisco, California, to the northwest section of Pocatello in the mid-1920s. The large cheese-processing plant took advantage of the capacity of southern Idaho's dairy farms to provide cheese products throughout the western United States. According to the *Chicago Tribune*, Kraft sold some 50 million boxes of its macaroni and cheese during World War II. The product was so popular because shoppers could purchase two boxes for one war ration stamp. (Courtesy of the Bannock County Historical Society.)

Young nurse cadets were trained at Saint Anthony's Hospital in Pocatello and then drafted into the service. On March 2, 1945, the director of nurses at Saint Anthony's, listed only as Sister Maureen, testified to Congress that young male nursing students were promised they would not be singled out and drafted when they entered the training program. Violations of that promise had apparently hindered efforts at recruiting males nurses, so Sister Maureen encouraged the government to keep its word. (Courtesy of the Bannock County Historical Society.)

Irving Junior High School, now Irving Middle School, opened in 1925 as one of two junior high schools serving the students of Pocatello. Built on the west side of the railroad tracks (Franklin Junior High School served Pocatello students east of the tracks), Irving's athletic field was constructed by the Civil Works Administration during the Great Depression and hosted football games for students from nearby Pocatello High School. World War II had a devastating impact on the education profession in Idaho and across the United States, as both students and teachers left school to enlist. According to the *Edvocate*, an online magazine, by 1944, only two thirds of the pre-war teaching force in the United States was still teaching. (Courtesy of the Bannock County Historical Society.)

Three

BY LAND

Taken on September 20, 1940, this image shows five men from the National Guard Armory Artillery. They are located near the Boise area and are in the field practicing with their equipment. The Idaho desert offered great areas such as this for military use because the vast fields of sagebrush ensured they had the space to train with weapons without endangering the lives of any of their men. In this chapter, the impacts of the US Army in Idaho during World War II will be explored. (Courtesy of the Idaho State Archives.)

Pictured here is Thomas Verd Murdock from Idaho Falls. Murdock joined the Army in 1944 and was stationed in Japan. He fought in the Battle of Manila in 1945, where he chased Japanese soldiers off the Philippine islands. It was in this battle that Murdock was bitten by a mosquito and contracted the malaria virus. He was expected to remain in the fight, so while his body raged against the parasite, Murdock stayed in the Army fighting for his country. (Courtesy of the *Idaho State Journal*.)

Two members of the Women's Army Corps are shown returning to Italy. On the left is Marjorie G. Byram from Twin Falls, formerly a member of the 1st WAC Company, HRPE. She later transferred to the 5th Army as a secretary in G-1 in Italy. On the right is Katherine M. Pyle, A-900201, of San Diego, California, who was a secretary for the general staff of the Allied Force Headquarters. (Courtesy of the National Archives.)

This booklet is from Pocatello High School's class of 1942. On each page, the graduates are listed with more information about them. The page pictured here mentions Paul Dudunake, a Pocatello resident who served in the Army from March 1943 until December 1945. (Courtesy of the Marshall Public Library.)

Donat, G. Robert, 1345 Lavine Drive, Pocatello. m: Alice Merrell. ch: Dianne 22, Terry 14, Jim 10. Service: Air Force, Corp., 1943-1946. Occ: Assistant Civil Engineer, U.P.R.R.

Douglass, Gerald A., 1722 Fourth Street, Cheney, Washington. m: Beverly Silverthorn. ch: Diana L. 18, Garth 13. Service: Air Force, Capt., 1942-44 and 1950 to present. Degrees: Bachelor of Science, University of Denver. Interests: Looking forward to retirement in 1968. Occ: U.S.A.F. presently in Southeast Asia. APO 96273, San Francisco, until November, 1967.

Downing, Patricia (Mrs. Pierce Bilyeu), 7800 Semeca Way, North Highlands, California. ch: Jay Downing 20, Charles "Chip" Pierce 13, Ann Marie 12. Degrees: Bachelor of Arts, Idaho State University. Housewife.

Dudenake, Paul, 1937 East Clark, Pocatello. m: Betty Farenges. ch: Michael 17, Paula 15, Karen 13, Kenneth 10. Service: Army, tank outfit, Pfc., March 1943-December 1945. Occ: Owner Emerald Club.

Dudley, Ora Jean (Mrs. Robert E. Harper), 5045 Chinook, Pocatello. ch: Patsy 21, Debora 15, Gail 9, Robert E, 11, 4. Interests: Extension courses at Idaho State University. Housewife and Mother.

Duerden, Artel (Mrs. Tom Donovan), 905 South Western Avenue, Anaheim, California. ch: Tom II 19, Melinda 15. Housewife.

Dunham, William P.

Edgley, Howard, 1239 East Wyeth, Pocatello. m: Shirley Cooper. ch: LeeAnn 21, Pamela 19, Elizabeth 17, Barbara 15, Beverly 12, Deborah 11, Craig 8. Service: Air Force, S/Sgt., August 1943-October 1945. Occ: Watchmaker.

Endow, Kazuo, 571 South, Blackfoot, Idaho.

Evans, Medabelle (Mrs. James O'Brien), 9664 Wampler Street, Pico Rivera, California. ch: Nancy 20, Karen 16, Bonnie 11. Interests: First grandchild due July 22. Housewife.

Exeter, Floyd, Army Education Center, A.P.O., New York, New York. m: Barbara Priest. ch: Sharon 17, Karel 14, Karen 13, Kim 11. Service: Army, Pfc., 1943-1946. Degrees: Bachelor of Arts, Idaho State College. Occ: Teaching (overseas presently).

Farmer, Dewey, Box 391, Linder Road, Meridian, Idaho. m: Helen Hansen. ch: Bob 27, Ann 24, Craig 16, Nyle 13. Service: Navy, AMM 1/C, June 1940-June 1946. Interests: Fishing. Occ: Deputy Marshall.

Fechtel, Robert P., 23 Ardmore Road, Worchester, Massachusetts. m: Betty Ginzel. ch: Ann M. 17, R. Brian 10. Service: Navy, SAD 3/C, August 1943-January 1946. Degrees: Bachelor of Science, Northwestern University. Occ: Banker.

Fernandez, Isabel, Regent 7-0882, New York, New York. Degrees: Registered Nurse. Occ: Nurse at Sloan Kettering Cancer Memorial Center.

Fernandez, Mary Carmen (Mrs. Willard K. Paulsen), 1926 LaCresta Drive, Salt Lake City, Utah. ch: Ronald Ray 19, Richard W. 16, Joseph Kristopher 12. Interests: State and local agencies in Mental Retardation as parent. Housewife.

Findlay, Vonda (Mrs. Vonda Nicholas), 478 Neil Drive, Yuba City, Calif. ch: Jim 23, Andrea 18, Dennis 19, Betti 16. Occ: Bookkeeper.

Flint, Helen J., 15332 S. E. Olive Avenue, Milwaukie, Oregon. Degrees: Bachelor of Arts, Washington State College; Master of Education, Oregon State University. Honors: Selected to attend NDEA Institute in Geography, Syracuse University, summer 1967. Occ: Teacher.

Foley, Jerry, 155 Chase, Pocatello. m: Arlene Hronek.

Foreman, Dr. Darhl L., Battles Road, Gates Mills, Ohio. Degrees: Ph D, Zoology, University of Chicago. Honors: Fellowship Hadley Univ.,

- 8 -

Class of 1942

Silver Memories

Class of 1942

1942~1967

WHO'S WHO?

39

Lt. Chester L. Freckleton enlisted in the Army two months after Pearl Harbor. During his service, he was George Patton's driver for a time before transferring to the Army Air Force and becoming a B-17 bomber pilot. (Courtesy of the Marshall Public Library.)

Lt. Ray Brookhart, an infantryman, was visiting his hometown of Pocatello before departing for overseas duty. Brookhart was the 1939 editor of Pocatello High School's yearbook, *The Pocatellian*. Brookhart went on to serve in the Korean War as well. (Courtesy of the Marshall Public Library.)

The man whose headstone application is seen here was Pfc. Garth Porter Beck. Private Beck was born and raised in Paris, Idaho, a town of approximately 500, nearly 6,000 feet above sea level in the furthest southeast corner of the state near Bear Lake and the borders with Utah and Wyoming. Beck was stationed in Okinawa, Japan, where he gave the ultimate sacrifice in the Battle of Okinawa. He died during medical treatment after the battle as a result of wounds he received. (Courtesy of Angie Willhelm.)

Pictured here are Lieutenant Shelton (left) and Lieutenant Thomas. Lieutenant Shelton played an important role in the war effort because he was a first operations officer. This likely means he was in charge of planning and training soldiers stationed in Pocatello. (Courtesy of the Marshall Public Library.)

Servicemen can be seen marching in a parade with their weapons over their shoulders. This was for a Fourth of July parade in 1942, which was surely a very patriotic time for Idaho and the town of Moscow, where the photograph was taken. Located in the rolling wheat fields of the Palouse country of northern Idaho, Moscow is the home of the University of Idaho. (Courtesy of the University of Idaho Special Collections.)

Two young men show their patriotism by dressing up as servicemembers for the Fourth of July parade in Moscow. Even though children may have had a less active role in the war effort than their adult counterparts, they still contributed greatly to the morale efforts through support and school war bond activities. It is important to remember that children were affected by the war through loss and separation. (Courtesy of the University of Idaho Special Collections.)

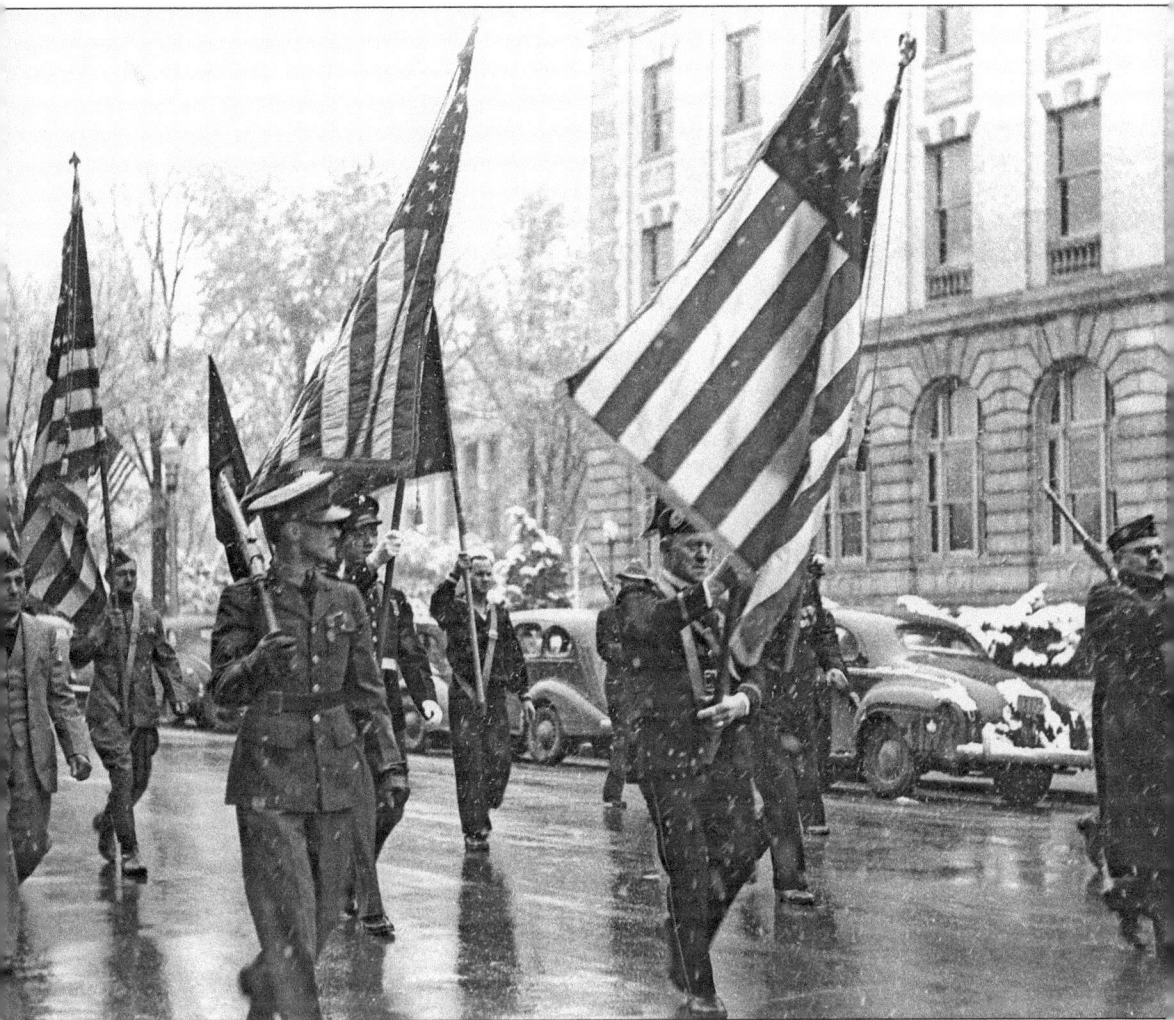

Armistice Day, now known as Veteran's Day, celebrates the armistice that was signed on November 11, 1918, to mark the end of World War I. This image shows the military color guard marching past the capitol building in Boise during an Armistice Day parade. Marching through town in the snow, these men celebrate a day that was supposed to prevent all wars in the future, just a year before they were to join the fight in World War II. (Courtesy of the Idaho State Archives.)

World War II veterans are pictured returning home. The end of the war brought its own challenges, as thousands of veterans returned to Idaho to resume their lives and train for careers. The Servicemen's Readjustment Act of 1944, better known as the GI Bill, was created to help with that transition. The GI Bill established hospitals, provided access to low-interest mortgages, and most importantly, granted stipends covering tuition and expenses for veterans to attend college or trade schools. Idaho's colleges benefited greatly from the influx of veterans after World War II. For instance, the Lewiston State Normal School grew into the Northern Idaho College of Education, and the University of Idaho Southern Branch in Pocatello became a four-year school, Idaho State College, to meet demand. (Courtesy of the *Idaho State Journal*.)

Four

BY SEA

Thelma Dixy, great-granddaughter of Chief Pocatello for whom the city of Pocatello was named, sponsored the USS *Pocatello*. When a woman sponsors a ship, she carves her initials into the keel of the ship, christens it, and is forever tied, at least in part, to the ship and its crew. The USS *Pocatello* was an artillery ship, and weighed over 1,100 tons. It could travel up to 20 knots, which is 23 mph. The ship was decommissioned in May 1946 and sold for scrap in 1947. It is the only ship to be named after Pocatello. This chapter discusses the US Navy presence in Idaho from the northern part of the state to the south. (Courtesy of the Marshall Public Library.)

This is an aerial view of Lewiston Normal School (now Lewis-Clark State College) and Zimmerly Air Transport around 1943. Zimmerly Air Transport was founded by Fred Zimmerly in 1934 to provide flight training and aeronautical services, including mercy flights in the wilderness of the Pacific Northwest. The CAA War Training Service was based here, and naval pilots were trained here during World War II to prepare for combat. This image showcases the hangar, main buildings, and planes located at the facility. (Courtesy of the Idaho State Archives.)

This S-6000-B Travelair seven-passenger airplane, pictured at the Zimmerly Air Transport School of Flying in Lewiston, was used for Civil Air Patrol and to help control forest fires. The Zimmerly Air Transport School worked in conjunction with Lewiston Normal School to train over 1,700 naval pilots without injury or death during the war. Founder Fred Zimmerly later worked as a pilot for Northwest Airlines and retired in 1970. (Courtesy of the Idaho State Archives.)

The US Navy began construction on Farragut Naval Training Center in Bayview, Idaho, on April 23, 1942. Farragut was built for a $58 million construction contract, awarded to Walter Butler Company of St. Paul, Minnesota, in just over three months with the labor of up to 7,000 workers on site. At the time of the attack on Pearl Harbor, the Navy had only three training facilities and realized that it had to quickly add capacity to train the thousands needed to serve on ships and shore installations. Farragut quickly became the second-largest naval training center in the country. (Courtesy of the Museum of North Idaho.)

Sailors from the Farragut Naval Training Center are in a Skippy Jr. boat in Coeur d'Alene, Idaho. The Desert Hotel can be seen behind the boat. They are on Lake Pend Oreille, the fifth-deepest lake in the United States. It was used for naval training at Farragut and early developments of submarines. Although Farragut Naval Training was disbanded shortly after the war, military submarine developments are still done at Lake Pend Oreille. (Courtesy of the Museum of North Idaho.)

During the war, women on the home front were unable to get nylons because of material shortages. Though it did nothing to warm their legs, they would draw on stockings with tanning lotion, then use an eyeliner pencil to draw a seam up the back. However, girls with beaus who were stationed at the San Diego naval base would frequently be sent gifts of nylons that their boyfriends bought in Mexico. (Courtesy of the Marshall Public Library.)

A Memorial Day parade in Coeur d'Alene is seen here, with sailors from the Farragut Naval Training Center. The parade began on Sherman Road and passed Dream Theatre, Shine's Place, the bus depot, Fritz's Corner, and the Sugar Bowl. (Courtesy of the Museum of North Idaho.)

Another group of sailors from the Farragut Naval Training Center marches in a Memorial Day parade through downtown Coeur d'Alene. They are between First Street and Sherman Road, with Lake Pend Oreille, Miller's Café, and the Victor Apartments visible in the background. The light jacket weather belies the extreme cold of winters in Farragut, where troops occasionally dealt with feet of snow on the ground and bone-chilling conditions from the spray off the lake. According to an article in the *Coeur d'Alene/Post Falls Press*, one of the trainees, Robert Adamson, admitted that he endured the cold temperatures while serving outdoor guard duty by setting an outside toilet on fire. (Courtesy of the Museum of North Idaho.)

Idaho State University is pictured in 1943. At the time this photograph was taken, it was still the Southern Branch of the University of Idaho. The building at front left is Gravely Hall, which was used for naval training and also housing for young cadets during World War II. (Courtesy of the Bannock County Historical Society.)

Dr. John R. Nichols worked as the executive dean for the Southern Branch of the University of Idaho around the World War II era. The editors of the college's yearbook, which during World War II was known as the *Dittybag*, dedicated the 1943 edition to Nichols, a veteran of World War I and a lieutenant commander in the US Navy. (Courtesy of the Marshall Public Library.)

Pictured at right and below is the steam plant that was in operation during the war and continues to heat Idaho State University today. It provides warmth for over 40 buildings, and 80 percent of the water from the steam is returned to be reused for more heat. Over two miles' worth of piping and tunnels run under the campus to move this steam. During World War II, it was in a different location, near the liberal arts building, and helped to heat the naval training base in Graveley Hall. After the war, it was relocated by what is now the Public Safety Office. (Both, courtesy of the Bannock County Historical Society.)

This is a photograph of a young man, Fred Roberts, coming back to Idaho to visit one of his high school teachers, Mr. Bond. Roberts served in the US Marines as a corporal but was stationed at the Naval Ordnance Plant in Pocatello. The plant was near the Union Pacific Railroad tracks so that large weapons and armor manufactured for naval ships could be easily shipped to the West Coast. (Courtesy of the Marshall Public Library.)

Pictured from left to right are Seaman Sid Wray, CPO Ray Stephens, and Robert Jensen, who was in the V-12 Navy Collegiate program. All three of these young men went to Pocatello High School, which is where this photograph was taken when they returned to their hometown to visit. (Courtesy of the Marshall Public Library.)

The two men seen here are PO Dennis Bale and Seaman Dean Hart. They are posing after reminiscing about their sports accomplishments at Pocatello High School. Hart served in the military for two years, primarily working on an aircraft carrier, the USS *Wasp*. (Courtesy of the Marshall Public Library.)

Gene Rutan from Nampa, Idaho, served in the Marine Corps, and his battalion was the first to travel on the *Queen Mary*. The ship was painted gray and nicknamed "the Grey Ghost." There were up to 16,000 men aboard the ship at any given time. (Courtesy of Gene Rutan.)

Navy officers are shown in front of a plane at Weeks Field. They were instructed in aerobatics by Gladys Buroker. According to the Smithsonian National Air and Space Museum, Buroker had a passion for aviation that was instilled in her at a young age. Through hard work and experience, she became the first female instructor at the all-male Saint Martin's College in the Civilian Pilot

Training Program. When World War II began, Buroker and her husband, Herb, started their own pilot training program in Coeur d'Alene, which they called Weeks Field. (Courtesy of the Museum of North Idaho.)

John M. Dudunake of Pocatello served with the US Marines. In a remarkable story shared by his family, Dudunake was badly injured in heavy fire and was believed to be dead. However, as the bodies of the deceased were being carted away, Dudanake made eye contact with the crew chief, who realized that Dudunake was still alive and saved him. Dudunake returned to the United States to reunite with his stunned and delighted parents, who had been notified (as published in *Life* magazine, below) that their son had been killed in action. Dudunake went on to live into his 90s and was even honored in person during a Mariners' game in Seattle for his bravery and service. He was also awarded the Purple Heart. (Both, courtesy of LuAnn Dudunake Spain.)

IDAHO

BASALT
Frandsen, Marvin E.
BOISE
Brenner, Walter James
Cahoon, Carol I.
Drake, J. Gordon
Eno, Griffith Edgar
Haynes, Curtis James
Kootlas, Frank
Maffett, Weyman Junior
Ragan, Robert E.
Ruscoe, Jackson
Sayre, Paul F.
Throckmorton, Lester Lee
Veeder, Gordon Elliott
BONNERS FERRY
Slater, Richard Carl
BUHL
Boyer, Albert George
BURKE
Cornelius, Dennis Vincent
Henslee, Everett W.
BURLEY
Jolley, Berry Stanley
COEUR D'ALENE
Boutillier, William A.
Crane, Cecil L.
Wofford, James M.
COLBURN
Doyle, James W.
COTTONWOOD
Jacobs, Richard William
DIETRICH
Gage, James Ferron
Lipe, Wilbur Thomas
DOWNEY
Hickman, Gene E.
FILER
Joslin, Raymond R.
FISH HAVEN
Jensen, Warren N.
FRUITLAND
Thomas, Leland E.
GENESEE
Dresher, James J.
Rosenau, Howard Arthur
GENEVA
Evans, William Orville
GRANGEVILLE
McGree Thomas Odle
HAGERMAN
Owsley, Thomas Lee
Weech, Miles
HOMEDALE
Goracke, William T.
IDAHO FALLS
Bagshaw, Kenneth P.
Genther, Adam
Loveland, Frank Crook
Nelson, Rex
JEROME
Briggs, Lyle Lee
Jackson, Oral B.
Rupert, Dale Elton
KELLOGG
Muller, Harry G.
KIMBERLY
Gentry, Wayne R.

Hall, William Stewart
Pendleton, Robert Clay
KOOTENAI
Stockman, Harold W.
LEWISTON
Balsley, Lucius M.
Koontz, Floyd Leonard
Williams, Edfred M.
MAY
Wayman, George
MAYFIELD
Evans, Eugene
MOSCOW
Cummings, George H.
MOUNTAIN HOME
Holden, Richard A.
NAMPA
Nielsen, Robert K.
Riner, Merrill W.
Sealey, Harry Albert
Zacek, Laddie John
NAPLES
Marcy, Gordon Wayne
McFarland, Burness C.
OAKLEY
Warr, Franklin O.
PARMA
Fisk, Harold R.
PAYETTE
Amack, Marvin Lee
Colton, Myron Dale
Deshazer, Larry E.
Kennard, Kenneth Frank
POCATELLO
Dudenake, John M.
Heath, Richard Gordon
Smith, Don A.
POTLATCH
Fiscus, Shirley H.
PRIEST RIVER
Anderson, John Alfred
Doyle, Ronald W.
RIGBY
Larsen, James Jay
RIRIE
Mason, Byron Dailey
RUPERT
Friesen, Kenneth C.
SALMON
Prosser, Stanley M.
SHELLEY
Bradley, Carl Merrill
SPIRIT LAKE
Beito, Jess
STERLING
Wright, Wilford D.
TWIN FALLS
Hyde, Blaine N.
Marsh, William Arthur
WALLACE
Henrickson, Gilbert David
WEISER
Cochran, Robert F.
Galey, William Francis
WINCHESTER
Hackwith, Emerson L.
Leader, Kent E.

Shown in this c. 1944 image is the family of John M. Dudunake. From left to right are (first row, seated) Ann Dudunake, father Michael Dudunake, son Angelo, mother Maria Dudunake, and Katharine Sakelaris with her son Mike; (second row) brother Harry Dudunake, John M. Dudunake, his wife June Dudunake, brother Paul Dudunake, niece Elaine Sakelaris, and brother-in-law George Sakelaris; (third row) sister Kris Strictland, brother Matt Dudunake, and sister Helen Dudunake. Parents Michael and Maria were immigrants from Greece. (Courtesy of LuAnn Dudunake Spain.)

John M. Dudunake and his wife, June, are pictured here. Both served in the Marines in World War II, and they met in Lakehurst, New Jersey, where John had been transferred and where June was packing parachutes. Making their home in Pocatello, John and June were the proud parents of nine children and had a 67-year marriage in which their days were filled with farming, travel, service work, and family. (Courtesy of LuAnn Dudunake Spain.)

Five

BY AIR

This map outlines the major areas in Bannock County around the 1940s. This chapter explains more about Idaho's direct influence on the war, especially with regard to pilots and bombers, many of whom were trained at the Pocatello Army Air Base. Pocatello provided more than just USO huts for soldiers during World War II; it was also a place where pilots were trained before flying over the Pacific to fight in combat. (Courtesy of the Marshall Public Library.)

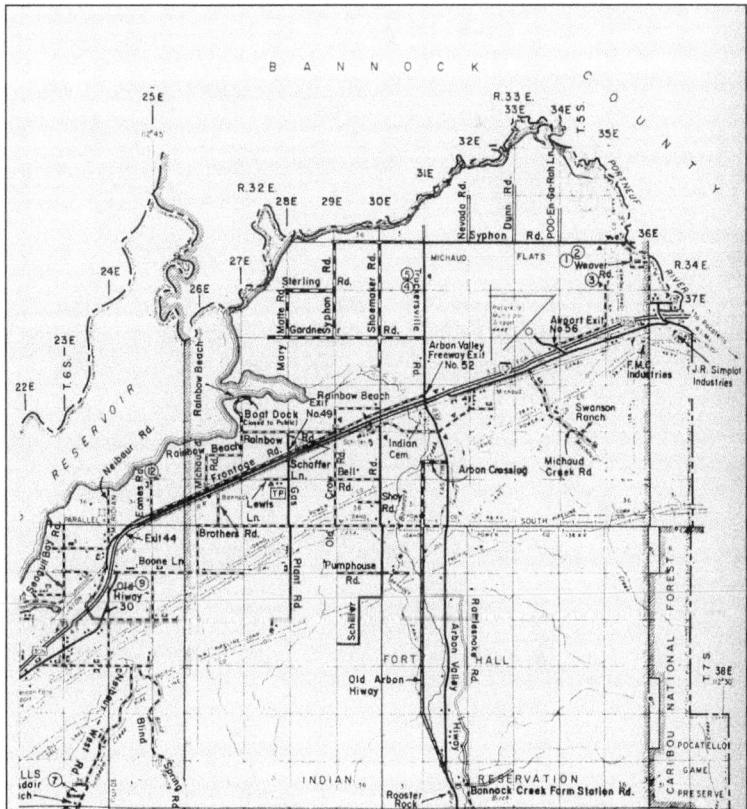

This image showcases buildings at the Pocatello Army Air Base in 1942–1943. These buildings may have served as barracks for soldiers stationed in Pocatello, or they may have been used as offices for military officials. According to the *Idaho State Journal*, around 40,000 military personnel were trained at the base during World War II. (Courtesy of the Marshall Public Library.)

Pictured here is the ramp and control tower at the Pocatello Army Air Base in 1942. At center, a plane taxis either to or from the runway. The air base was in a more isolated area of Bannock County and the Pocatello area, but it was very alive with soldiers and technicians during World War II. (Courtesy of the Marshall Public Library.)

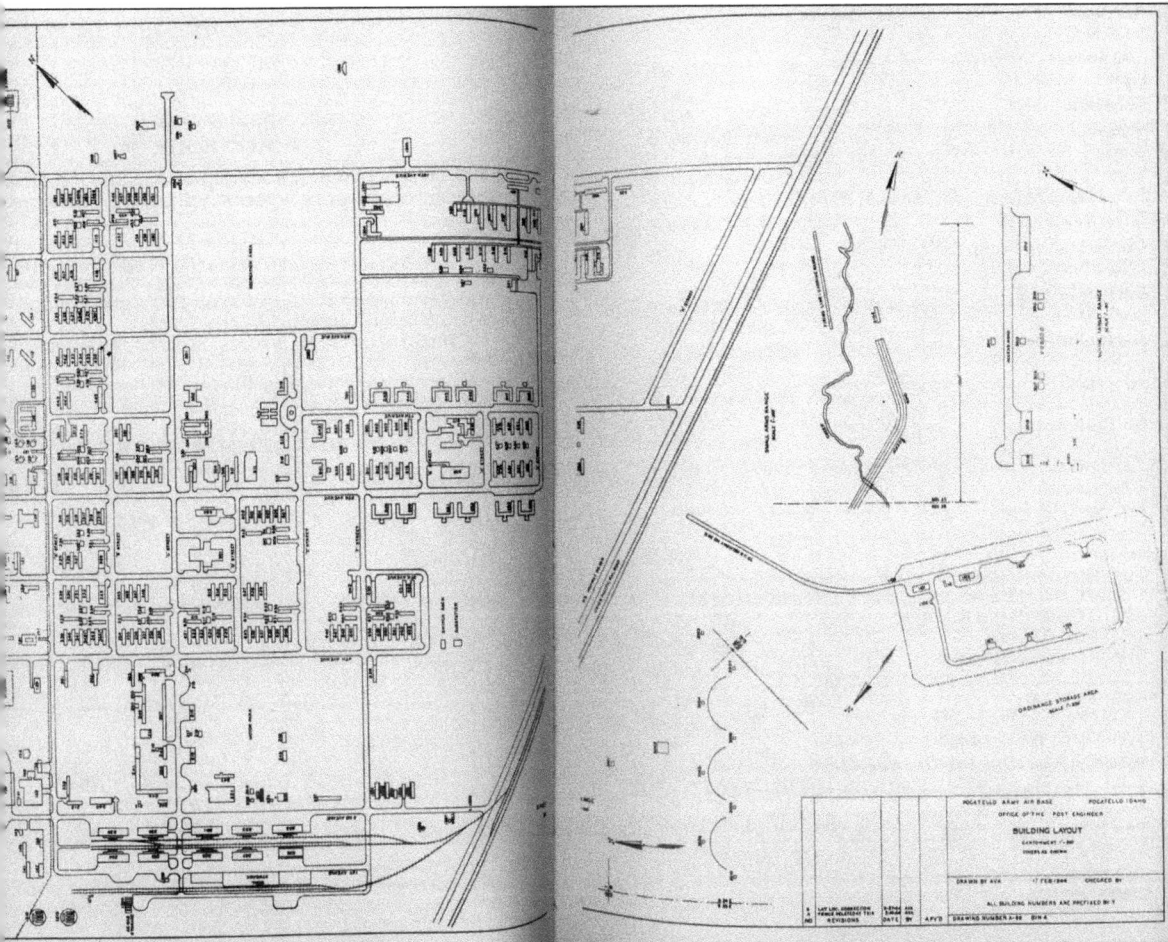

This map outlines the layout of the Pocatello Army Air Base in 1944. The base had a target range for practice with small firearms, a recreation area, barracks for soldiers, and a motor park. US Highway 30, which runs parallel to what is now Interstate 86, and the Union Pacific Railroad also traversed through a section of the base. (Courtesy of the Marshall Public Library.)

As pilots approached the air base, they would pass over the Union Pacific Round House, which is shown here. According to the authors of *The First Fifty Years: Michaud Flats U.S. Army Base, Pocatello Regional Airport*, pilots would use this building to gauge how close they were to the base in Pocatello. (Courtesy of the Marshall Public Library.)

This is the emblem for a training squadron stationed at the Pocatello Army Air Base in 1944. The 72nd Fighter Wing was a bomb squad, and its insignia and emblem, appropriately, was an eagle grasping a bomb in its talons. (Courtesy of the Marshall Public Library.)

This image shows the traditional clothing, brightly decorated with fringes and feathers, of the people native to the Great Basin lands of southern and eastern Idaho. Originally, the land that the Pocatello Army Air Base was built on had been part of the Fort Hall Reservation, which had been set aside for the Shoshone Bannock Tribes. After the war, the air base land was turned over to the City of Pocatello and became the new Pocatello Regional Airport. (Courtesy of the Marshall Public Library.)

A fighter is pictured at the Pocatello Army Air Base. The pilot stopped for a quick refuelling, and then most likely headed back into the air, possibly to travel to another base in the United States. Airplanes were a key technological aspect of World War II. (Courtesy of the Marshall Public Library.)

Two officials stationed at the Pocatello Army Air Base are seen here. According to *The First Fifty Years*, the man on the right was special affairs officer Lt. Kelly. He played an important role at the base because he welcomed people visiting. One of the people he greeted was Andy Devine, a famous actor. Devine was well known for his acting in Western movies; one of his more popular roles was Cookie, Roy Rogers's sidekick. (Courtesy of the Marshall Public Library.)

This image from 1943 shows a group of men at the Pocatello Army Air Base. Although the names of the soldiers pictured here are not listed, the men served in the engineering section of the 732nd Bomb Squadron. They played an important role in maintaining the bomber aircraft flown in World War II. (Courtesy of the Marshall Public Library.)

Pictured here is the "model" crew stationed at Pocatello. This group served as the example for others training at the base. From left to right are (first row) Barr, Johnson, and Wilkins; (second row) Wattenberger, Martin, Trout, and Schaff. (Courtesy of the Marshall Public Library.)

This image from 1943 showcases the Communication Section of the 732nd Bomb Squadron stationed at the Pocatello Army Air Base. These men played an important role in relaying information between pilots during training. Effective communication was paramount for successful combat strategy in World War II. (Courtesy of the Marshall Public Library.)

Pictured here are the transportation personnel who worked at the Pocatello Army Air Base. According to the authors of *The First Fifty Years*, the man in the center at front was the staff sergeant, the "slickest" card dealer at the base. The Pocatello Army Air Base was constructed just two miles west of the site of Pocatello's first municipal airport, McDougall Field, which had been constructed in 1929 near Michaud Flats and was named in honor of Harry McDougall, a World War I flying ace who died in an air show accident in Pocatello in 1928. (Courtesy of the Marshall Public Library.)

CONFIDENTIAL

I. ORGANIZATION AND ADMINISTRATION

In December, Pocatello Army Air Field's mission of training fighter pilots for the Army Air Forces was discontinued, and Second Air Force Headquarters reported the field as surplus to Headquarters Army Air Forces.[1]

Following instructions received on 12 December 1944 from 72nd Wing Headquarters,[2] there was set in motion, therefore, a procedure for the inactivation of this station for stand-by status. Pocatello Army Air Field thereafter became a transient air base according to the provisions of Par. 2A, Section X, Part II, AAF Manual 55-1 (Inactivation Manual).

At the same time 72nd Wing requested that Headquarters Pocatello Army Air Field see "that buildings and grounds be put in proper state of repair and police by 20 December and that report of completion of that action to this headquarters be made."[3]

When this mission was accomplished, Pocatello Army Air Field and all Second Air Force Units stationed thereat were relieved from assignment to the 72nd Fighter Wing and placed under the direct jurisdiction

---

[1] CONFIDENTIAL TWX 72W 702, CG, FIWG 72, to CO, PAAF, 11 Dec. 1944.

[2] CONFIDENTIAL TWX 72W (C) GP 774, CG, FIWG 72, to CO, PAAF, 12 Dec. 1944.

[3] Confidential TWX 72W 702, CG, FIWG 72, to CO, PAAF, 11 Dec. 1944.

CONFIDENTIAL

This document from 1944 relates to the Pocatello Army Air Base. The document, which used to contain classified information, explains how the air base was disbanded, and fighter pilot training was halted. Second Air Force units were actually stationed at the base as well, but because it was disbanded, they were required to move elsewhere. The air field transitioned from a space designed for war preparation to a "transient" air base known today as the Pocatello Regional Airport. (Courtesy of the Marshall Public Library.)

Pictured here is a Canadian training plane at the Pocatello Army Air Base. According to the authors of *The First Fifty Years*, aircraft like this were used primarily for training purposes during World War II. (Courtesy of the Marshall Public Library.)

Weeks Field in Coeur d'Alene was the first municipally-owned airport in the United States. During World War II, it became a War Training Service facility. Critical contributions to the training of pilots were made there. This photograph shows some of the instructors at Weeks Field in 1944 in front of a plane used for training. (Courtesy of the Museum of North Idaho.)

This classroom at Weeks Field was used for training, mapping out routes, and ensuring pilots were equipped with the skills and knowledge they needed. From left to right are Earl Pitts, Lew Aristonic, Glenn Johnson, Jim Doyle, Curt Anderson, and an unidentified man and woman. Clay Henley is at the blackboard. (Courtesy of the Museum of North Idaho.)

Flight instructors from Aviation Industries at Weeks Field are standing in front of a two-engine Cessna UC-78 Bobcat. The Cessna Flyer Association reported that metal, particularly aluminum, was in scarce supply at the time. Consequently, new Bobcats were made largely of wood, which led to their common nickname of Bamboo Bombers. From left to right are Cal Dawson, Joe Westover, Clay Henley, Herb Munro, Earl Pitts, Emerson Duffield, and Earl Potter. (Courtesy of the Museum of North Idaho.)

Due to its ideal climate and geographic isolation provided by the Rocky Mountains, Idaho was chosen as the perfect location for an air base in the capital city of Boise. Costing over $2 million, this base was to include housing, storage, administration, and of course, training areas for an estimated 2,500 people. Boise Air Base was renamed Gowen Field in 1941 to honor a fallen pilot, Paul Gowen, from Caldwell. This base remained quite active during World War II, offering a convenient location for combat planes to land and refuel. After the war, the Idaho Air National Guard began leasing the land from the city in order to keep this base active and keep the runways open for the Boise community. (Courtesy of Gowen Field Memorial Park.)

Shown here on the left is Edward Frederick Lindley Wood, first earl of Halifax, also known as Lord Halifax. Lord Halifax was a decorated British politician, holding positions before World War II as viceroy to India and Britain's foreign secretary. A supporter of Prime Minister Neville Chamberlain's appeasement policy toward Germany and the Nazi regime, Halifax changed his mind after Germany invaded Poland. During the early 1940s, Halifax served the important post of British ambassador to the United States. It was in this role that he met with US military personnel stationed at Gowen Field in Boise. (Courtesy of the Library of Congress.)

A P-80 jet fighter is pictured at Gowen Field. This single-seat fighter was developed to match the technology being developed by Germany during World War II. The P-80 made its first appearance at the very end of World War II. However, it and subsequent jet fighters became very important during the Korean War in the 1950s. (Courtesy of the Idaho State Archives.)

This photograph provides an aerial view of Gowen Field in Boise. According to Seth Husney from the National World War II Museum, Boise's temperate climate, proximity to major western cities, and geographic isolation made Gowen Field an ideal location for a training base. The base specialized in training crews for the B-17 Flying Fortress and B-24 Liberator. (Courtesy of the Idaho State Archives.)

This photograph by Leo J. Leeburn at a Gowen Field airshow shows an early P-80 Shooting Star jet fighter. According to Lockheed Martin Corporation, Lockheed chief engineer Kelly Johnson and an elite team were commissioned to develop this fighter in response to German jet fighters that were superior to US aircraft in both speed and acceleration. The team was given a lofty deadline of 150 days to design and build the new aircraft. Thanks to their dedication, they finished seven days early. (Courtesy of the Idaho State Archives.)

Mechanics are working on a radial engine for a B-17 bomber at Gowen Field. All units of the Idaho National Guard were active during World War II, and it was an all-hands-on-deck situation. Every person was important to the cause, whether their skills were in supporting roles, such as mechanics, or in the battle itself. (Courtesy of the Idaho State Archives.)

Aviation was still relatively new in the 1940s, and airplanes were far from reliable. In fact, according to the National Park Service, over 7,100 plane crashes occurred on American soil during World War II, and this only includes the aircraft that were part of the US Army Air Force. These crashes were responsible for the loss of over 15,500 lives. This photograph shows one such crash in front of a house in Boise. (Courtesy of the Idaho State Archives.)

Bradley Airport was on part of what had been the Goodman Ranch on Highway 20, two miles northwest of Boise. Ground was broken for the airport at the very end of World War II and initial construction was completed in July 1946. The airport was dedicated to Frederick Worthen Bradley, a highly successful mining engineer whose career spanned from the 1860s gold rush in California to mines in Idaho in the 1920s that were only accessible via airplane in the winter. Bradley Airport was quite expansive, with a 3,000-foot-long gravel runway that was later paved. Other improvements included airplane hangars, tie-down service, a motel and cafe on site, and a parts department. It remained open until the early 1970s. Today, the campus of Vineyard Church in Garden City occupies part of the former airport property. (Courtesy of the Idaho State Archives.)

This image shows a B-24 D bomber from the World War II era. According to Forest Garner, more B-24s were built than any other multi-engine airplane at the time. The B-24 had 60 different variations, powered by four 14-cylinder air-cooled Pratt and Whitney R-1830 Twin Wasp engines. The B-24 D could hold up to 8,000 pounds of bombs. (Courtesy of the Marshall Public Library.)

The "Pocatello Chief" B-24 bomber was named after Chief Pocatello, the namesake of the city in southeastern Idaho. This bomber was delivered to the 8th Air Force in England for combat in 1943. Unfortunately, it was shot down over enemy territory in 1944. (Courtesy of the Marshall Public Library.)

Pictured here are two planes flying in the skies over southern Idaho in the early 1940s. The Mountain Home Air Base, 40 miles southeast of Boise, was the third of the three Army air bases to open in southern Idaho during World War II. Opened in August 1943 as a training base for bombers, Mountain Home was listed as inactive in 1945 following the Allies' victories in Europe and the Pacific. However, Mountain Home was reopened in 1948 by the US Air Force, which was newly independent of the Army in the aftermath of World War II. (Courtesy of the Marshall Public Library.)

Pictured here are four members of the Air National Guard. From left to right are Lt. A.H. Bode, Lt. Harold Hansen, Capt. William G. Foster, and Sgt. A.G. Hylent. The men are wearing their flight suits and standing in front of a biplane. According to the *Encyclopedia Britannica*, biplanes were much more prevalent during World War I, and after World War II, they were mostly used for crop dusting and aerobatic flight. (Courtesy of the Idaho State Archives.)

The airplanes in this photograph were designed for cross-country flight. Whenever these planes needed to land at night, kerosene lanterns were used to light the dark runways. Electric lighting of runways in a rural state such as Idaho was generally not feasible during World War II, so kerosene lanterns, despite their significant potential risks, were the best option. The only other option was lining up cars and turning on their headlights. (Courtesy of the Museum of North Idaho.)

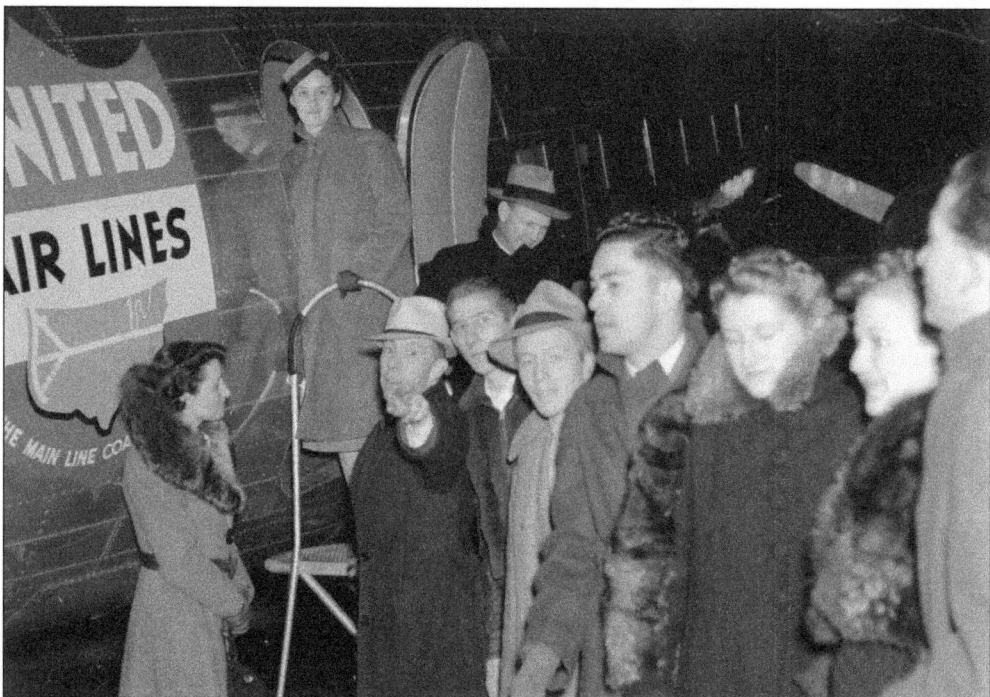

Taken in 1939, this photograph shows the first United Airlines mainline aircraft. According to the United Airlines official historical timeline, the company's first flight (under the name Varney Airlines, after company founder and aviation pioneer Walter Varney) took off on the morning of April 6, 1926, from Pasco, Washington, to Boise. United went on to become the first airline to create a flight kitchen. During World War II, United broke ground by including women in many parts of the aviation industry as opposed to only hiring them as flight attendants. (Courtesy of the Idaho State Archives.)

The United Airlines Historical Foundation describes how the company's first flight, piloted by Leon Cuddeback, carried almost 10,000 pieces of mail, which weighed over 200 pounds. Crowd after crowd appeared at each stop on the flight route, including one in Boise, for the public to celebrate the accomplishment. Thirteen years later, on the brink of World War II, this photograph shows Postmaster Henry L. Yost receiving a bag of mail in Boise. (Courtesy of the Idaho State Archives.)

This photograph shows employees of United Airlines at the original Boise Airport, Booth Field, during Air Mail Week. Booth Field was built in 1926 on a gravel bed near the Boise River on land close to what is now the campus of Boise State University. According to the American Air Mail Society, Postmaster General James A. Farley and President Roosevelt created this weeklong event in observance of the 20th anniversary of the first regularly scheduled air mail service in the United States. Shown here are United Airlines officials posing beside a plane in May 1938. (Courtesy of the Idaho State Archives.)

This is a member of the "Aztec Eagles," a Mexican fighter squadron composed of 300 volunteer pilots. These men came to the United States for training in 1944, with their first stop in Texas, but eventually moved on to continue their training at the air base in Pocatello. El Squadron 201 combined forces with an Army Air Force group, and spent almost 1,300 hours in flight time during their missions fighting alongside the Allies to remove Japanese troops from islands in the Pacific. The Aztec Eagles officially returned from the war on November 18, a day on which this squadron honors its fallen men. (Courtesy of the National Archives.)

One Step
Nearer Victory

We are happy to have had a vital part in the construction of the Air Base Cantonment at Pocatello. Through its completion and use as a training base, we are assured of being one more step nearer victory.

We wish to express our appreciation to all contractors and their personnel and to all participating firms with which we were associated during construction of the base.

We join with all Pocatellans in extending a cordial welcome to all U. S. officers and men who will be stationed here.

Vernon Bros. Company
CONTRACTORS
Eighth and Orchard   Boise

This advertisement was placed in the *Pocatello Tribune* in 1943 by the Vernon Brothers Company of Boise. Vernon Brothers was an example of an Idaho-based company that served as a local contractor for a number of aviation-related national defense projects during the war. For example, Vernon Brothers collaborated with the US National Defense Program in 1941 to make essential improvements to the Baker City, Oregon, municipal airport and leveraged that experience to contribute to the construction of the army air base in Pocatello. After the war, Vernon Brothers branched out from aviation construction to contribute to other kinds of projects in Idaho, including reinforcing the Black Canyon Canal near Caldwell, Idaho, and installing machinery and equipment in the Anderson Ranch Power Plant on the Boise River near Mountain Home. (Courtesy of the Marshall Public Library.)

The Civilian Pilot Training Program was initiated by President Roosevelt at the end of 1938 to prepare the United States for air combat in case of war. All told, 193,000 new pilots entered the US Army Air Forces during World War II. The rapid opening and expansion of air bases throughout the United States, however, put pressure on housing inventory and the infrastructure of local communities. This image shows one of the officers from the Pocatello air base with his wife in front of the house on Fourth Street in Pocatello where they were renting a room. (Courtesy of the Bannock County Historical Society.)

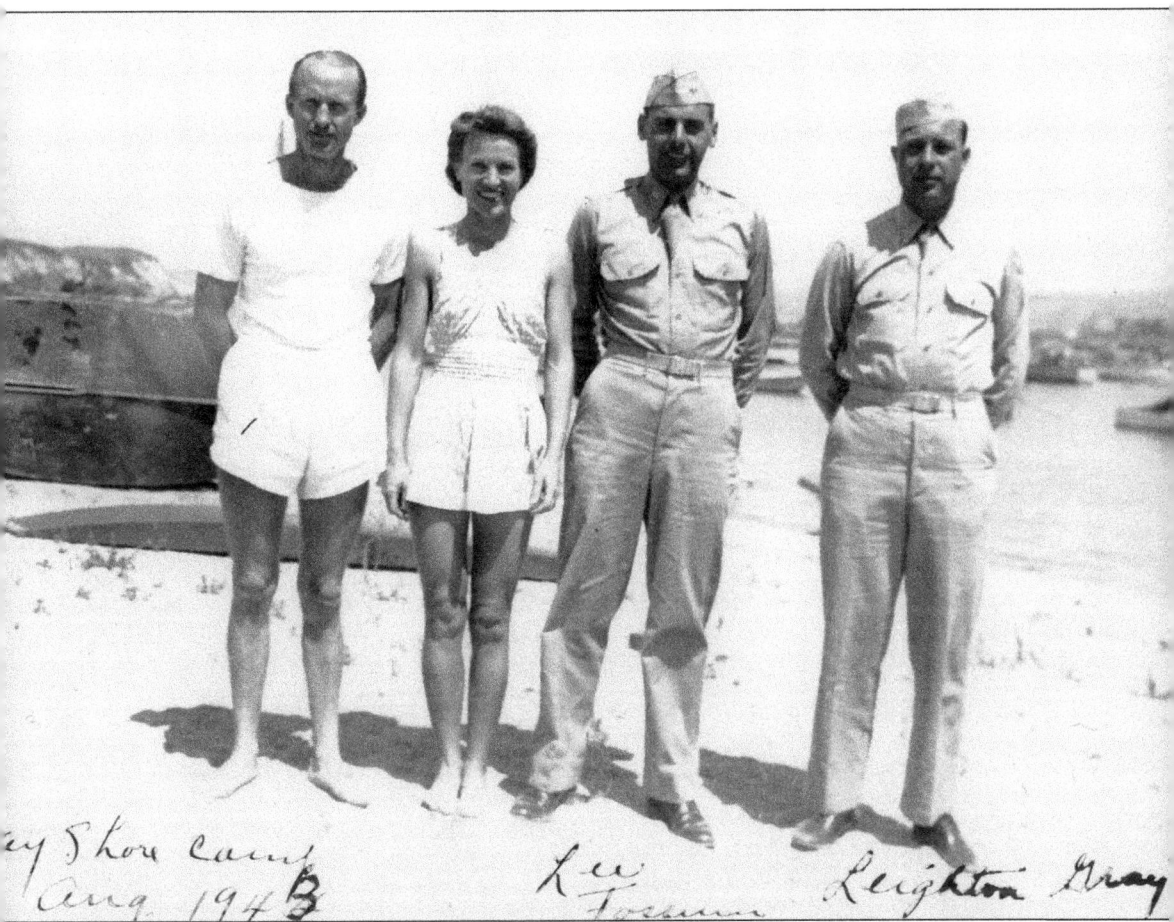

y Shore camp
aug 194B *Lee* *Fossum* *Leighton Gray*

Soon after Lee M. Fossum (second to right) attended the University of Idaho, Pearl Harbor was attacked. According to Fossum's obituary in the *Spokesman-Review*, he joined the Army Air Corps and did training at Geiger Field in 1942. He became a bombardier on a B-17 Flying Fortress. He flew 30 missions and was shot down in one of them. He survived the crash, though he sustained a back injury. After recovering, he returned to being a bombardier and was honorably discharged when the war ended in 1945. (Courtesy of the Museum of North Idaho.)

HEADQUARTERS NINTH SERVICE COMMAND
OFFICE OF THE COMMANDING GENERAL
FORT DOUGLAS, UTAH

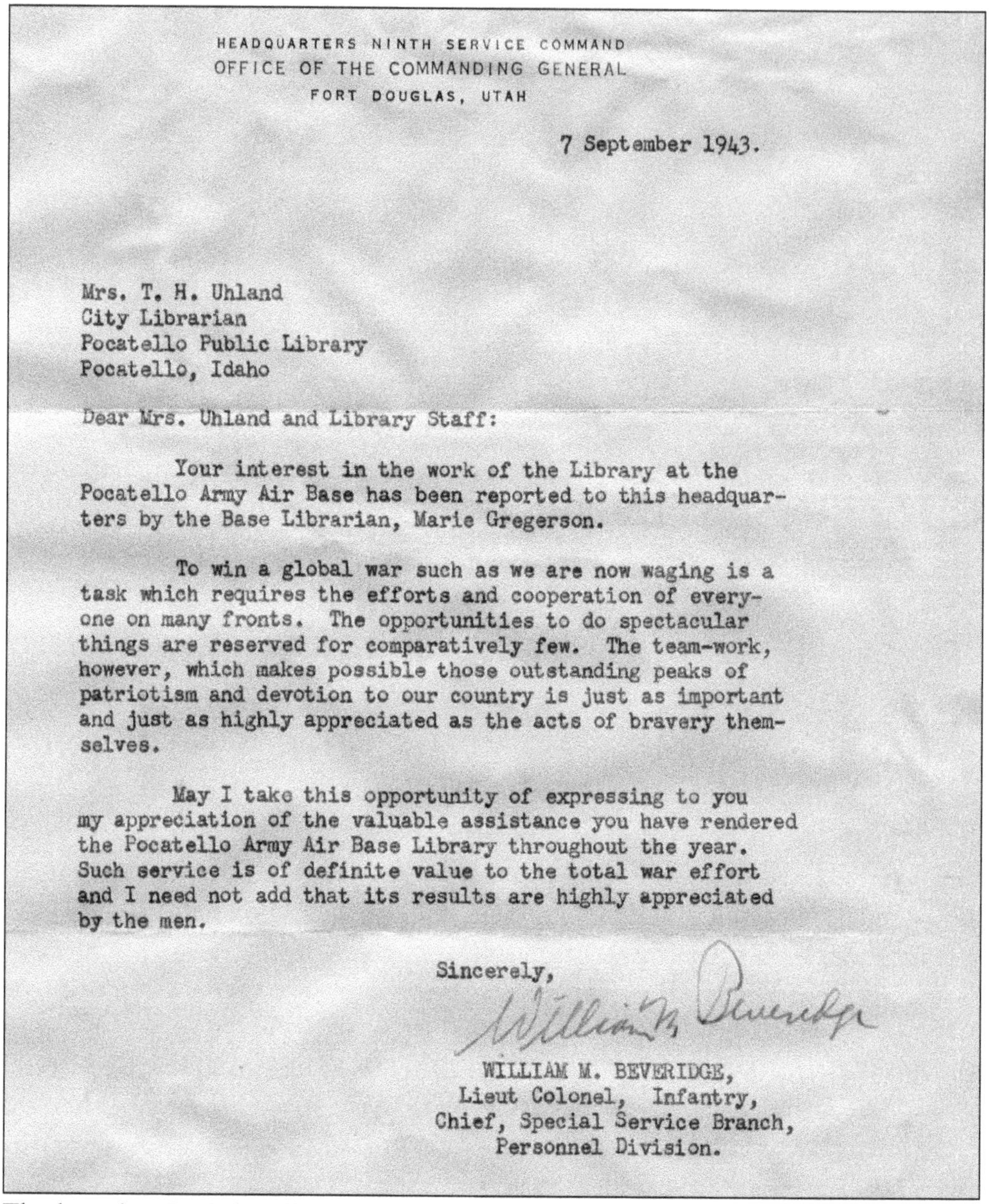

7 September 1943.

Mrs. T. H. Uhland
City Librarian
Pocatello Public Library
Pocatello, Idaho

Dear Mrs. Uhland and Library Staff:

Your interest in the work of the Library at the Pocatello Army Air Base has been reported to this headquarters by the Base Librarian, Marie Gregerson.

To win a global war such as we are now waging is a task which requires the efforts and cooperation of everyone on many fronts. The opportunities to do spectacular things are reserved for comparatively few. The team-work, however, which makes possible those outstanding peaks of patriotism and devotion to our country is just as important and just as highly appreciated as the acts of bravery themselves.

May I take this opportunity of expressing to you my appreciation of the valuable assistance you have rendered the Pocatello Army Air Base Library throughout the year. Such service is of definite value to the total war effort and I need not add that its results are highly appreciated by the men.

Sincerely,

William M. Beveridge

WILLIAM M. BEVERIDGE,
Lieut Colonel, Infantry,
Chief, Special Service Branch,
Personnel Division.

This letter from Lt. Col. William Beveridge thanks Mrs. T.H. Uhland from the Pocatello Public Library for her help in establishing a library at the Pocatello Army Air Base. Libraries at military bases were a helpful part of keeping up morale in young men who could be serving thousands of miles away from their homes and in need of something to enjoy, such as a good book. Some of the more popular books at the time, including *For Whom the Bell Tolls* by Ernest Hemingway, *The Stranger* by Albert Camus, and *A Tree Grows in Brooklyn* by Betty Smith, were likely available for soldiers to read at the library while training in Pocatello. (Courtesy of the Marshall Public Library.)

Six

MINIDOKA WAR RELOCATION CENTER

Japanese American citizens were involuntarily detained at the Minidoka War Relocation Camp near Jerome, Idaho, during World War II. Seven months before Pearl Harbor, a Japanese American stood before Congress and read this document. In it, the patriotism that the Japanese American man felt for his country was evident, especially when he explained how the country had given him opportunities and freedoms that he could not have found elsewhere. According to the *Densho Encyclopedia*, some Americans have conflicting emotions about the content of this creed; even so, it is an important document to consider when examining the history of our country at the time. (Courtesy of the Idaho State Archives.)

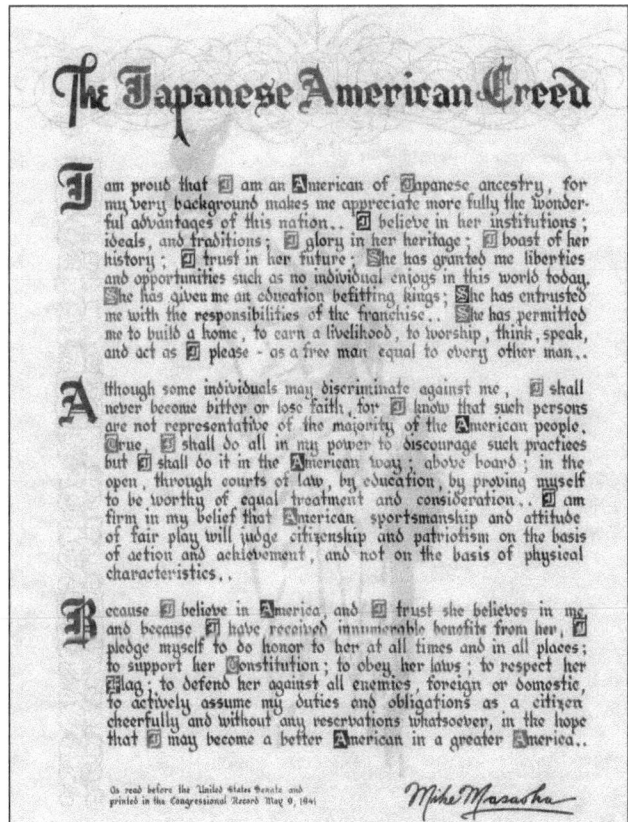

The Japanese American Creed

I am proud that I am an American of Japanese ancestry, for my very background makes me appreciate more fully the wonderful advantages of this nation.. I believe in her institutions; ideals, and traditions; I glory in her heritage; I boast of her history; I trust in her future; She has granted me liberties and opportunities such as no individual enjoys in this world today. She has given me an education befitting kings; She has entrusted me with the responsibilities of the franchise.. She has permitted me to build a home, to earn a livelihood, to worship, think, speak, and act as I please - as a free man equal to every other man..

Although some individuals may discriminate against me, I shall never become bitter or lose faith, for I know that such persons are not representative of the majority of the American people. True, I shall do all in my power to discourage such practices but I shall do it in the American way; above board; in the open, through courts of law, by education, by proving myself to be worthy of equal treatment and consideration.. I am firm in my belief that American sportsmanship and attitude of fair play will judge citizenship and patriotism on the basis of action and achievement, and not on the basis of physical characteristics..

Because I believe in America, and I trust she believes in me, and because I have received innumerable benefits from her, I pledge myself to do honor to her at all times and in all places; to support her Constitution; to obey her laws; to respect her Flag; to defend her against all enemies, foreign or domestic, to actively assume my duties and obligations as a citizen cheerfully and without any reservations whatsoever, in the hope that I may become a better American in a greater America..

As read before the United States Senate and printed in the Congressional Record May 9, 1941

Mike Masaoka

85

This is an aerial view of the buildings at the Minidoka internment camp. According to Theresa Tamura in her book *Minidoka*, the barracks measured 20 by 120 feet, and contained six apartment units in each building. The barracks were organized into blocks, and 36 blocks made up the entire camp. The apartments inside the buildings were small and crowded, especially because most of the families lived together in their single unit. (Courtesy of the Densho Digital Repository.)

The camp spanned three miles across Jerome County in southern Idaho. This image shows the entrance to the camp, which was closely monitored by guardsmen. According to the sign at right, inspections and paperwork were required for those entering the relocation center. (Courtesy of the Densho Digital Repository.)

These children are working on an art project in the Minidoka camp. The photograph shows how adaptable young people can be. It was not only adult Japanese Americans who had their entire lives uprooted by the relocation effort, but also the children who were taken away from their homes, schools, and friends. (Courtesy of the Densho Digital Repository.)

Japanese Americans from all walks of life were in the Minidoka internment camp, including children who resided with their parents. Most of them, like the children pictured here eating in the mess hall in 1944, did not understand why they were in the desert instead of their homes on the coast. Children were required to attend the Minidoka Project School, which was run by teachers selected by the War Relocation Association. (WRA). (Courtesy of the Densho Digital Repository.)

These Japanese Americans worked as lifeguards at the Minidoka Relocation Center. Although a large amount of time in the camp was spent working in the fields, there were some recreational moments as well. The detainees had the option to swim in irrigation canals nearby, and as a result, young men were able to work as lifeguards. (Courtesy of the Densho Digital Repository.)

The group of men pictured here are Nisei, second-generation Japanese Americans. Many Nisei in the Minidoka Relocation Center volunteered to fight for their country in the war. According to the National Archives, the group pictured here are brothers who promised their father that, if given the opportunity, they would go to war for America. (Courtesy of the Densho Digital Repository.)

Japanese Americans could leave the Minidoka Relocation Center by volunteering for military service. The group pictured here are lining up for physicals. The Minidoka Relocation Center had the highest ratio of military volunteers out of all the centers on the West Coast. (Courtesy of the Densho Digital Repository.)

A Japanese American fires a gun on the front lines in Italy. This man was a member of the 100th Infantry Battalion, which, according to the *Densho Encyclopedia*, was the first group made up entirely of Japanese Americans to fight in combat during World War II. (Courtesy of the Densho Digital Repository.)

A squad of Japanese Americans is pictured at a camp on the front lines in Italy during 1944. The soldiers were huddled around a campfire, cooking a meal. According to the original caption on the photograph from the WRA, this squad would trade the flour they were issued with other groups of American soldiers for rice. (Courtesy of the Densho Digital Repository.)

This baseball game was played at the Tule Lake concentration camp in California. Baseball was an important aspect of life at all of the war relocation centers, including Minidoka. According to the original WRA captions, they had organized baseball leagues, and many of the detainees at the camp would come to watch the games. The games presented an opportunity for Japanese Americans to distract themselves from the hardships around them and, according to a report from KMVT news in Twin Falls, Idaho, served as a "glue" that brought the detainees together as a community. (Courtesy of the Densho Digital Repository.)

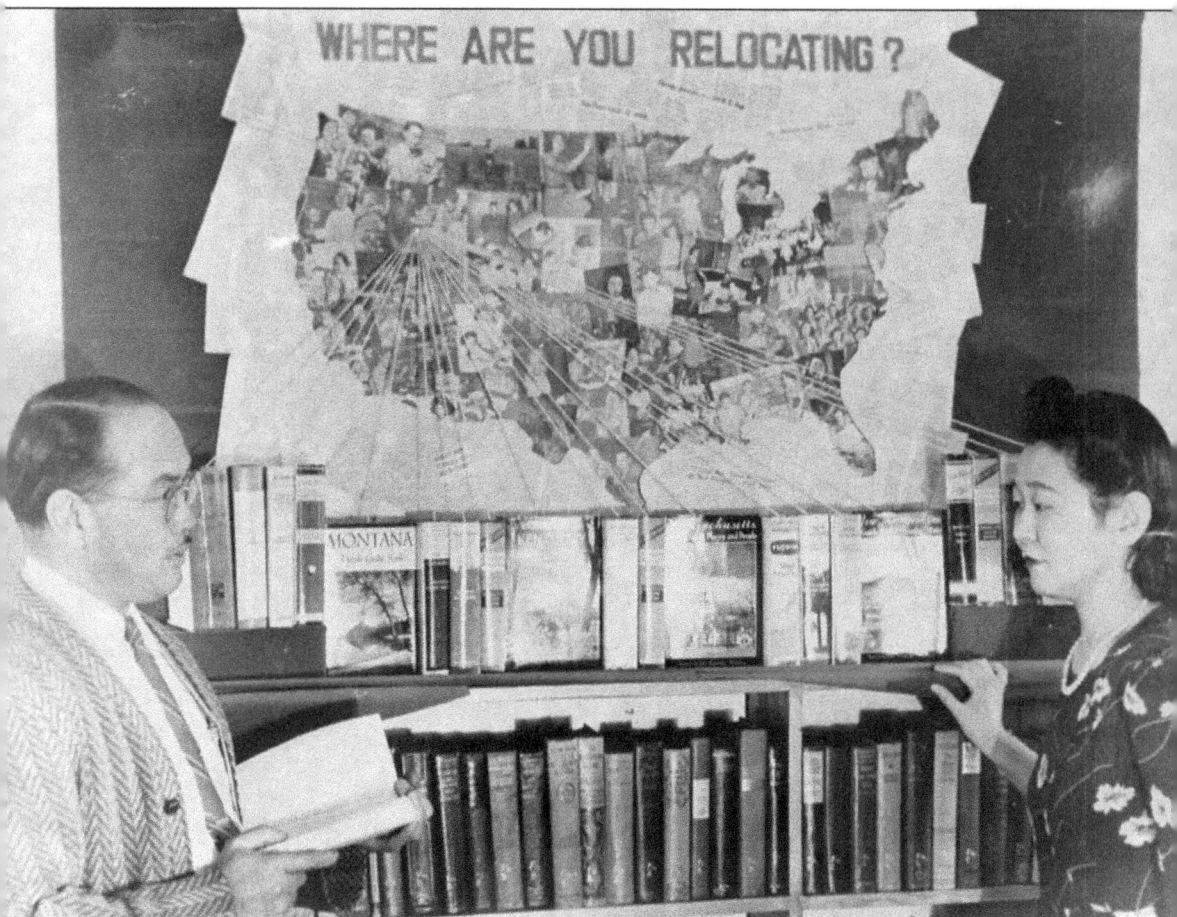

WHERE ARE YOU RELOCATING?

The Minidoka internment camp had a library that was accessible to Japanese Americans at the camp. This photograph shows a display in the library that points out different areas in the United States where Japanese Americans could relocate to after the Supreme Court ruled that they were allowed to leave the camps in 1945. Although the detainees had the option to return home, many of their original properties had been ransacked, so they had no home to return to. (Courtesy of the Densho Digital Repository.)

Some Japanese Americans at Minidoka were relocated to other camps across the country. This image from 1943 shows two people saying farewell as one prepares to leave on a train. According to the original WRA description, this train was carrying 254 Japanese Americans to the Tule Lake Center in California. For some detainees at the camps, this farewell would be the last time they would see each other. (Courtesy of the Densho Digital Repository.)

A large portion of life at the Minidoka Relocation Center was farming. This image shows a group of detainees from the camp working on a celery crop. There was a general labor shortage across the country as a result of the war, so many detainees were required to work on farms. (Courtesy of the Densho Digital Repository.)

Although life at the center was focused on work, there were elements of peace and relaxation as well. The Kogita garden is seen here. This was a place of relaxation and clarity for Japanese Americans at the camp, and included unique rock sculptures with cultural significance for the detainees. (Courtesy of the Densho Digital Repository.)

This is a memorial from the Mountain View Cemetery in Pocatello. It shows the names of Nisei soldiers who gave their lives for America during World War II. Japanese Americans served their country to the best of their ability, and some even gave their lives for the war effort. They did this even with their families at home in internment camps. The bottom of this memorial reads, "For our tomorrow, they gave their today." (Courtesy of Alex Bolinger.)

This is the baseball field at Minidoka today. These images make it possible to understand what life was like during World War II. It is necessary to acknowledge the suffering of the Japanese Americans who were detained, while also recognizing the historical impact of the Minidoka Relocation Center itself. (Courtesy of the National Parks Service.)

Seven

CIVILIAN LIFE

During the war, there were still many joys of civilian life. Here are a couple of girls strapped in and ready to enjoy a ride at the Patrick Traveling Carnival. The 1893 World's Fair in Chicago had over 27 million attendees and sparked the beginning of traveling shows; by 1936, it was estimated that 300 different carnivals were traveling the country to keep the people entertained. This chapter discusses what life on the home front was like for those who were not serving in the military and exemplifies the idea that life goes on no matter what. (Courtesy of the Idaho State Archives.)

GARFIELD

Tommy Barrett

As a result of gas rationing and various additional war-related factors, many rodeos were replaced with women's ranch events, barrel racing, and beauty pageants. However, the Pocatello Rodeo began in 1942 with the intent to entertain military personnel stationed at the Pocatello Army Air Base. The rodeo was known as the Victory Rodeo for the first three years. (Courtesy of the Bannock County Historical Society.)

This image shows a bowling alley during the war, with advertisements hanging along the back wall. Even though businesses were greatly affected by the war, and their production processes changed due to rations, they still moved on and proceeded to provide products and services to people. (Courtesy of the Bannock County Historical Society.)

During the latter years of the Great Depression and the early years of World War II, minor league baseball was an important source of entertainment and distraction in Idaho. The six-team Pioneer League initially included four teams from Idaho: the Boise Pilots, the Lewiston Indians, the Twin Falls Cowboys, and the Pocatello Cardinals. Two of these teams were affiliated with a team from Major League Baseball. The Pocatello Cardinals (at left and below) were part of the St. Louis Cardinals farm system. The Twin Falls Cowboys were originally affiliated with the New York Yankees. However, with so many young men drafted, the Pioneer League had to suspend operations from 1943 until the end of the war. (Both, courtesy of the Bannock County Historical Society.)

This photograph was taken October 18, 1940, during a high school football game, just 14 months before the United States' entry into World War II. Boise High School was playing Idaho Falls High School, which means a 280-mile commute (one-way) for the game. Sports remained important during the war to those on the home front, and these recreational activities helped relieve some of the tensions from the war. (Courtesy of the Idaho State Archives.)

Pictured here is the Spud Bowl at the Academy of Idaho, built in 1936. A few decades later, in 1970, Holt Arena was built as the new football stadium, which is located on the upper campus at Idaho State University. The Spud Bowl was later renamed Davis Field after one of the presidents of the university. This stadium is still widely used today for soccer, track and field, and various intramural sports. (Courtesy of the Bannock County Historical Society.)

The Saint Teresa's girls' basketball team of 1939 is seen here. According to the *Idaho Statesman*, Saint Teresa's Academy was the first high school in Boise and was founded by the Sisters of the Holy Cross in 1890 to educate young women. St. Joseph's was built for men soon after, and in 1933, the schools were combined to form a coed academy. In the 1960s, Saint Teresa's was succeeded by Bishop Kelly High School, which still exists in Boise. (Courtesy of the Idaho State Archives.)

These women are showing off their athleticism during the war. While many young men were leaving to serve their country, women's activities flourished. These photographs are from the *Pocatellian*, the yearbook for Pocatello High School, and include archers, ping pong players, and golfers. (Courtesy of the Marshall Public Library.)

These girls are taking a break to pose for a photograph at Frank's Roller Rink. Owned by Frank Holtzclaw and located at 712 Idaho Street in downtown Boise, Frank's Roller Rink capitalized on the so-called "golden age of roller skating" between the late 1930s and 1950s. Roller skating rapidly gained popularity as the top American participatory activity during World War II, because it was a convenient, inexpensive way to relieve stress and make social connections. In 1945, Frank's Roller Rink was open from 8:00 p.m. to 11:00 p.m. and offered instruction for those who needed it. (Courtesy of the Idaho State Archives.)

In December 1942, Bogus Basin, a ski resort just outside of Boise was opened to the public with a 500-foot rope tow to get skiers up the mountain. This photograph shows skiers waiting in line for the rope tow. (Courtesy of the Idaho State Archives.)

A charter bus of sailors from the Farragut Navy Training Center is in front of the Lookout Pass Ski Area sign. In the middle of the group is Lt. (jg) Jim M. Howard. They are enjoying the Idaho mountains. In 1941, the US Forest Services commissioned the Civilian Conservation Corps to build an expanded lodge at Lookout Pass that is still in use today. (Courtesy of the Museum of North Idaho.)

Above, Bertha Allsberry and her daughter Patty excitedly watch the ducks on the duck pond at Sun Valley Resort. Nestled in the Sawtooth Mountains of central Idaho under the shadow of Bald Mountain (below), Sun Valley was the first destination winter resort in the United States. It was developed by Averell Harriman, the chairman of the Union Pacific Railroad. Seeking to capitalize on the popularity of the 1932 Winter Olympics in Lake Placid, New York, Harriman sought to replicate the kind of ski resorts found in the Alps of Europe as a destination for travelers on the railroad. Sun Valley became famous in 1941 with the success of the movie *Sun Valley Serenade* (which featured Olympic figure skater Sonja Henie, Hollywood legend Milton Berle, and bandleader Glenn Miller). World War II hit winter tourism hard, however, and Sun Valley was converted to a convalescent hospital for the US Navy in 1942. (Above, courtesy of Patty Bolinger; below, courtesy of Alex Bolinger.)

This is a modeling photograph of Mary Lou Shaw, but at the time it was taken, her name was Mary Lou Simpson. This was before she met her husband-to-be in Sun Valley while he was on leave from the Navy. They married in 1947. Both civilians and service members alike sought distraction from the war in a variety of ways, and it is amazing that these two found love during this troubling time. (Courtesy of the Idaho State Archives.)

During the 1940s, KEIO radio in Pocatello operated out of the Bannock Hotel, not far from the Union Pacific Railroad station in what is now Old Town Pocatello. In an era before television, radio was a primary source of information about the war and world affairs. In 1951, KEIO became KWIK, which still operates as an AM station serving eastern Idaho. (Courtesy of the Bannock County Historical Society.)

Radio was the primary form of mass communication during World War II. Many households owned a radio by the early 1940s, and families gathered around their radio for information about the war, other world news, and entertainment. In what appears to be a promotional photograph from the mid-1940s, Don Headrick of the sheriff's department in Boise is shown using the radio. (Courtesy of the Idaho State Archives.)

Two young men are shown holding up fish they caught in front of the *Idaho Statesman* newspaper offices in Boise. In the harrowing months leading up to and during World War II, updates on the war were posted on the board behind them for residents of the Treasure Valley. The photograph was taken in August 1941, just three months prior to the bombing of Pearl Harbor and the United States entering World War II. (Courtesy of the Idaho State Archives.)

The Chief Theatre in Pocatello was built in 1938 and was open for more than 40 years before burning down in 1993. The front of the building shows that the comedy *Tovarich* was playing. During the war, movie theaters would play newsreels before the feature film that would update the public on the conflict overseas. They also showed advertisements asking people to purchase war bonds and grow victory gardens. Movies were a great opportunity for civilians to keep up their patriotism and support for the war as well as a welcome distraction from the stress of life where those they loved could be giving the ultimate sacrifice at any moment. (Both, courtesy of the Bannock County Historical Society.)

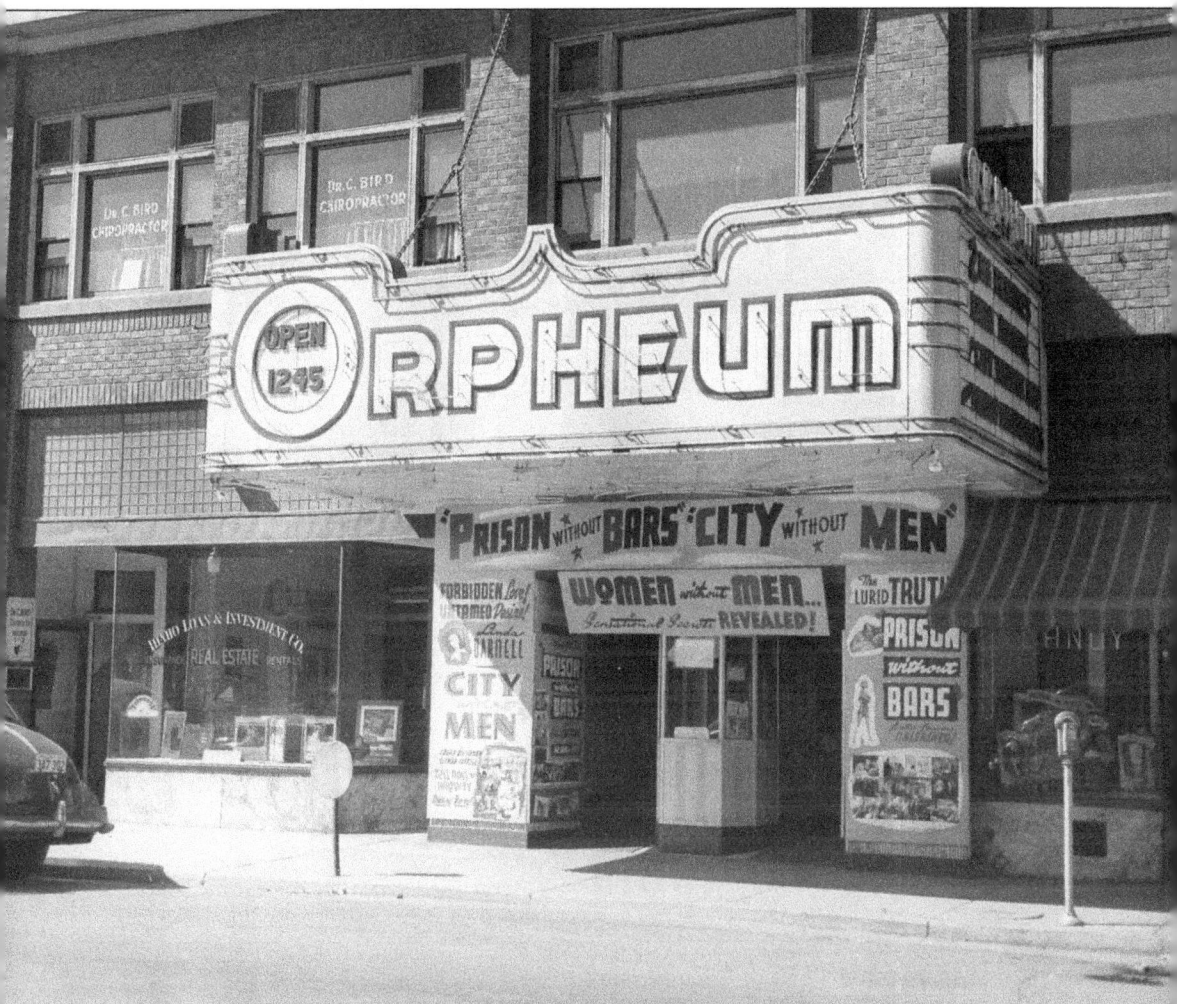

The Orpheum Theatre in Pocatello (pictured) was destroyed by fire in the 1970s, but its namesake 120 miles to the west in Twin Falls remains a treasure for theater-goers. Twin Falls's Orpheum Theatre, built in 1921 and renovated in 2014, and Joslin Field at Magic Valley Regional Airport (named after Sergeant Raymond Joslin, the first airman from Twin Falls County killed during World War II) are two Twin Falls institutions whose names and structures bear witness to the World War II era in the Magic Valley. (Courtesy of the Bannock County Historical Society.)

Yet another theater in Pocatello, the Rialto, sat on the 400 block of East Center Street between Bistline Lumber and the Ben Franklin five-and-dime. Bistline Lumber was established by John Bistline, an early mayor of Pocatello. His granddaughter Beverly joined the US Navy in Washington, DC, as a member of its Women Accepted for Volunteer Emergency Services program. After the war, she was one of the few women to earn her law degree at the University of Utah. Ben Franklin was one of the first franchised chain stores in the United States. It specialized in selling arts and craft materials, among other useful items. At one time, the Rialto (previously known as the Rex Theatre) held seating for over 600 patrons and a 2/4 Style B Wurlitzer theater organ. The large number of theaters speaks to their importance during the war. (Courtesy of the Bannock County Historical Society.)

The Wilson Opera House and Theatre presented various acts and performances from its opening in 1920. The Wilson, as it is known locally, is located in Rupert Square in downtown Rupert, Idaho, within 50 miles of the Minidoka War Relocation Camp. As this photograph shows, wartime news and propaganda made its way into every part of American life in the 1940s, including through the arts and theater. (Courtesy of the Idaho State Archives.)

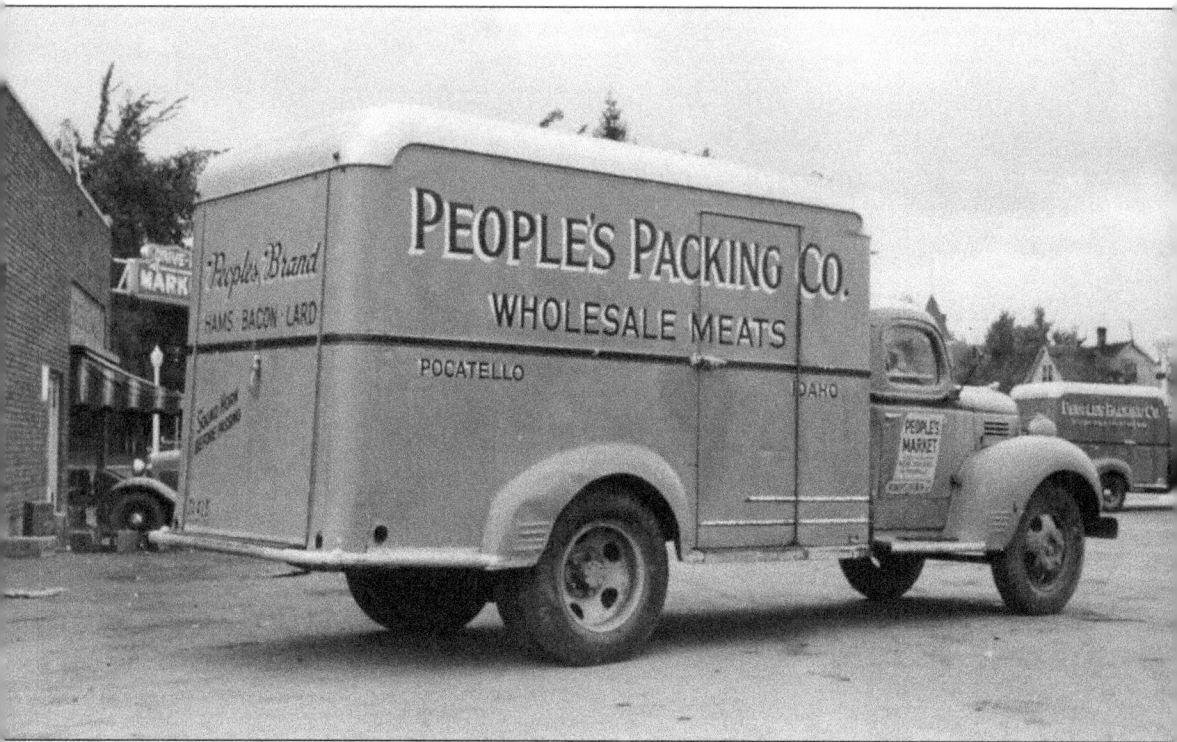

This truck was used in Pocatello for the People's Market, which was open from 1914 until 1963. Many markets were greatly affected by the war, especially in the form of rations. Stores had a hard time keeping shelves looking well-stocked because any surplus supplies were going to the troops. This played a large part in the development of superstores that sell more than groceries because they began to stock non-food items so the shelves looked less barren. (Courtesy of the Bannock County Historical Society.)

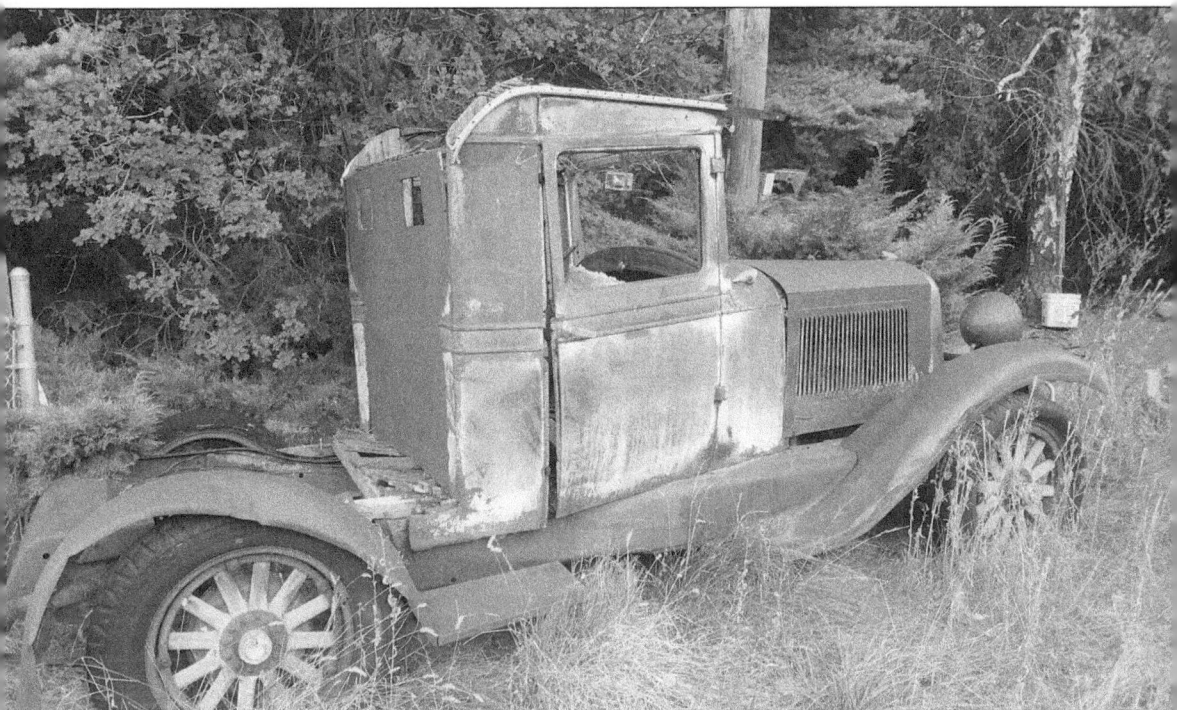

This is a recent photograph of a Studebaker truck, currently owned by a man in the Twin Falls area. The joint where it was welded between the cab and the truck bed can be seen here. This was due to the fact that during the war, people could not purchase fuel for a car, only for a truck. This was to keep fuel available for the troops. This law caused a number of these conversions to be done to all sorts of vehicles. Additionally, there was no private vehicle production or sales between 1942 and 1946, by government order. (Courtesy of Dale Hunter.)

Pictured here are some of the firefighters who served in Boise during World War II. Due to the labor shortage caused by the war, it was difficult for civil service organizations like fire and police departments to keep enough able-bodied men on staff to respond to emergencies. Fear about enemy soldiers setting off domestic wildfires reached its peak in February 1942, when a Japanese submarine shelled the Ellwood Oil Field near Santa Barbara, California. In response, the US War Advertising Council created Smokey the Bear to raise the public's awareness of their role in preventing wildfires. (Courtesy of the Idaho State Archives.)

A sailor and woman are shown crossing Sherman Avenue at Second Street in Coeur d'Alene. They are directly in front of the Wilma Theatre, which was known as the Huff Theatre before 1940. The theater seated 600. Dream Theatre is on the right, used for live theater and shows. Also shown are Central Motors and a Texaco station. (Courtesy of the Museum of North Idaho.)

Pictured here is Main Street in Boise, looking to the west. Taking place June 17–19, 1940, the street is decorated with banners and flags to celebrate the Idaho Marches On! event. Businesses on the left (south) side of the street include, from front to back, Sampson Music, Lyric Theater, Western Union, Club Cigars, and the Owyhee Hotel. On the right (north) side are Potter Drug, Green-Griffin Co. Jewelry, Globe Optical, and the Idanha Hotel. (Courtesy of the Idaho State Archives.)

North Eighth Street in Boise is now a residential area, but before World War II, it was a central hub for business. The amount of traffic decreased drastically in the years after this photograph was taken, as gasoline rationing dictated that fuel could only be purchased for vehicles that were used primarily for work. (Courtesy of the Idaho State Archives.)

Young men who drove for Diamond Cab Company in 1940–1941 are seen here. Before the war, companies like this had just started to flourish after recovering from the Great Depression; however, they did not get to continue for long because the war not only took young workers out of employment, but also limited supplies due to rationing. (Courtesy of the Bannock County Historical Society.)

This image was taken in 1940 and shows the beautiful Payette Lake in McCall, Idaho. Not pictured, however, is Sharlie, the infamous lake monster. According to the McCall Chamber of Commerce, the first sighting of this creature was in 1920 by a crew of railroad workers. The crew claimed to have seen a large log in the lake that began moving on its own, creating a wake in the water. Another sighting in 1940 saw the supposed monster retreating into the depths. In 1944, another group saw the creature, describing it as "at least 35 feet long, with a dinosaur-type head, pronounced jaw, humps like a camel, and shell-like skin." At the time, the monster was referred to as "Slimy Slim," and it was not until 1954 that she was renamed "Sharlie" based on a line by Jack Pearl in a well-known radio show. Regular sightings of Sharlie continue to be reported today, and many McCall residents are true believers in their town's mysterious lake creature. (Courtesy of the Idaho State Archives.)

In 1942, when the war started, there were just under 600 African Americans in Idaho. During the war, that number grew by over 50 percent, partly attributable to the stationing of military personnel from around the country at various bases throughout the state. The war had a lasting effect on diversity within Idaho, as people from all parts of the country united to serve together. (Courtesy of the Bannock County Historical Society.)

This photograph shows a group of the Women of the Moose (WOM), a branch of the Loyal Order of the Moose. This fraternal organization was founded in 1888, with the female chapters beginning in 1913. According to Moose International, the WOM "provides social, educational and community service opportunities to its members, as well as sporting events and activities geared toward the entire family." (Courtesy of the Marshall Public Library.)

Visit us at
arcadiapublishing.com

www.ingramcontent.com/pod-product-compliance
Lightning Source LLC
Chambersburg PA
CBHW061235150426
42812CB00055BA/2595